# Abide In Me

# Abide In Me

Being Fully Alive In Christ

DOUGLAS J. EARLY

WIPF & STOCK · Eugene, Oregon

ABIDE IN ME
Being Fully Alive In Christ

Wipf & Stock
An Imprint of Wipf and Stock Publishers
199 W. 8th Ave., Suite 3
Eugene, OR 97401

www.wipfandstock.com

PAPERBACK ISBN: 978-1-4982-9111-8
HARDCOVER ISBN: 978-1-4982-9113-2
EBOOK ISBN: 978-1-4982-9112-5

Manufactured in the U.S.A.                                      08/01/16

For Andrea, Bronwyn and Ben—without whom, being fully alive would not be possible.

# Contents

# Permissions

# Preface

Years ago I read a line from John Calvin that sparked in my mind so powerfully it felt like an electrical current ran through my body. Calvin wrote, "When Christ is preached, the Kingdom of Heaven is opened to us so that being raised from death we may live the life of God."[1] Some days, I'll confess, I'm lucky to be raised from bed. So as I read this line, I stopped and pondered whether I really believed this to be true—not in a theoretical way but in a shake-up-my-life-and-cause-my-family-to-worry-for-my-sanity kind of way. As I looked back, I realized that through the years I had been fortunate enough to be "raised from death" by the words of certain preachers and teachers who opened my soul to an electrifying awareness of the presence of the living God.

Since I preach on a regular basis, this line from Calvin also caused me to evaluate whether I was doing the same for my own congregation—"opening the Kingdom of Heaven" in a way that "raised them from death" to live life in full. Unfortunately, I realized that some Sundays I was lucky just to raise a few people from sleep. Yet Jesus calls us all to far more than somnambulism.

At about the same time as I read that line from Calvin, I was lucky enough to find another preacher who opened the kingdom of heaven to me, who helped raise me from death, to live, at least more than before, the life of God. That *preacher* was the Apostle John. When reading John's First Letter, I found a person who spoke in a way that awakened my soul. His images, his personality,

1. Calvin, *Commentaries*, 160.

and his thought processes opened the door on my slumber and led me into the fuller light of day.

Not wanting to keep this good news to myself, I preached a series of sermons from 1 John to the congregation of Queen Anne Presbyterian Church in Seattle, the church I serve as pastor. Over several months, the congregation and I received inspiration from John's letter. What follows in the pages of this book got its start in those days of study and reflection. As I have given John's words additional scrutiny and reflection in the process of writing this book, I have become even more convinced of the value of John's wisdom for our time.

One of the main reasons why I believe John's wisdom is helpful to people in our age can be summed up in a line of thought I once heard Eugene Peterson share in a class at Regent College. Peterson asserted that most of us don't need any more "information" in our lives, what we need is "transformation." Alain de Botton notes in his book, *The News: A User's Manual*, "More data flows into the [European control room of one global news organization] in a single day than mankind as a whole would have generated in the twenty-three centuries between the death of Socrates and the invention of the telephone."[2] And virtually all that same data can be accessed by anyone with a smartphone within seconds. As a consequence, I would venture to guess that many of us, at least at times, feel buried under this avalanche of information. So, I offer this book in hopes that God might use it as one of the means to help lift readers from this rubble of data. I offer this book in the hopes that God might use it in your life to open the door to the kingdom of heaven. I pray that these pages might help you share more in the life of God.

The good news in all of this is that the hard work has already been done. Experiencing the fullness of life that God desires for us is not a matter of us lifting ourselves out of the avalanche of information in order to find God. Nor is it a matter of finding new disciplines or working harder at the ones that we already know.

---

2. Botton, Alain de, *The News: A User's Manual*, Vintage International Edition, New York: Random House, Vintage 2014.

## Preface

John reminds us that kingdom of God is already with us, even within us. John witnessed Jesus raised from death to new life. John himself heard the words from Jesus that provide hope for us all. If we want to be fully alive, Jesus says, "Abide in me." It is not a matter of finding something new or working harder than ever before. It is a matter of attending to what already is.

One final note about gender in language throughout this book. My quotations of scripture come almost entirely from the NIV translation. I use this version primarily because it is the version our congregation had in the pews before I even started there. While the newer version has made progress in removing many of the male, gender-specific nouns and pronouns that need not be specific, they have not yet made it as far as I would like. In addition, several of the authors I quote also used male, gender-specific nouns and pronouns in their original writing that might be written differently today. I have tried to be respectful of the translation and authors I quote while at the same time being gender-inclusive whenever I am writing in my own voice. However, I know that I fall short even in my awareness of situations that might offend. So, I apologize for any and all of the writing that isn't as inclusive as it could or should be.

# Acknowledgments

All writing emerges from a specific context; and all published writing emerges from a context of significant support. Therefore, I would like to thank several people who have been significant supporters of this particular author and book.

Most of all I would like to thank my family. To Andrea, thank you for your care, your strength and your love. Without you, I'd probably be holed up in a dark room, unkempt, and wary of the world. With you, I have learned the content of the words "love" and "joy." To Bronwyn and Benjamin, thank you for your love. In being your dad, I experience purpose and sheer delight. To my own parents and my parents-in-law, the breadth of your support through the years and even to this day, humbles me. Thank you.

I also owe a debt of gratitude to Regent College and several pastors who have mentored me along the way. Before beginning my Master of Divinity program I had heard from numerous pastors that their time at seminary was one of the driest spiritual times of their lives. At Regent, I had the exact opposite experience. It was with the guidance of professors at Regent that I encountered the rich tradition of spirituality flowing through the church's history and its manifold expressions. At the same time, while interning at University Presbyterian Church in Seattle, both Lee Burkhart and Earl Palmer provided wonderful examples of pastors balancing work and life. Thank you.

To Wipf and Stock Publishers, thank you for providing me the opportunity to share this work with others.

## Acknowledgments

Finally, I would like to thank the congregation of Queen Anne Presbyterian Church. Your kindness to me and my family through the years has helped me glimpse the kingdom of God. I treasure being your pastor. Thank you.

Chapter One

# A Substantial Faith

*That which was from the beginning, which we have heard, which we have seen with our eyes, which we have looked at and our hands have touched —this we proclaim concerning the Word of life. The life appeared; we have seen it and testify to it, and we proclaim to you the eternal life, which was with the Father and has appeared to us. We proclaim to you what we have seen and heard, so that you also may have fellowship with us. And our fellowship is with the Father and with his Son, Jesus Christ. We write this to make our joy complete. (1 John 1:1–4 NIV)*

If a trusted friend or mentor offered me a sure way that I might experience *life* and *joy*, I think I'd hear them out. If I saw a commercial on late night TV offering me a "sure way" that I might experience *life* and *joy*, I wouldn't bother calling the 1–800 number. I think most of us are fairly cynical when it comes to sure-fire promises about our future. We are all too accustomed to hyperbolic sales pitches. What persuades most of us that something is true is tangible *evidence* or, in the hypothetical case of me and my trusted friend, the integrity of the person making the offer.

For many people these days, the promises Christianity makes seem about on par with those hawking ways to "Pay no taxes!

Ever!" If conversations drift toward matters of faith, they know to set up their cynic's defenses. Even many of us who have had a significant experience of Christ and who earnestly try to be his disciple can find ourselves unconvinced that Christ's presence in our lives will make a substantial difference.

And yet Christianity still has the gall to make the pitch. Witness John's claim in what the canonical scriptures number as his first letter:

> That which was from the beginning, which we have heard, which we have seen with our eyes, which we have looked at and our hands have touched—this we proclaim concerning the Word of life. The life appeared; we have seen it and testify to it, and we proclaim to you the eternal life, which was with the Father and has appeared to us. We proclaim to you what we have seen and heard, so that you also may have fellowship with us. And our fellowship is with the Father and with his Son, Jesus Christ. We write this to make our joy complete. (1:1–4)

Life and joy—John claims we can have more of both.

He starts with promising life. And not just the ordinary sort. These days, with the incredible advances we've seen in science and medicine, the whole cell-division, heart-beating type of life is becoming fairly run-of-the-mill, or run-of-the-petri-dish. John speaks of something qualitatively different. John speaks of "eternal" life. John speaks to us of a quality of life that makes our current existence pale in comparison.

The life we experience on a regular basis is one marred by our fallen nature. This is the life we experience when we yell at our kids in the morning, "Hurry! We're late!" This is the life we experience when we wake up in the middle of the night because we're not sure how we're going to get enough money to pay for the cleanup of our flooded basement. This is the life we experience when we hear our spouse say, "I'm leaving you." It is a life scarred by impatience and disappointment, by cruelty, greed, and violence.

In contrast to the life we normally experience, John promises the kind of life that John Calvin, the 16th century church reformer, speaks of as the "life of God." He means that we will share in God's life. In his typical bold fashion, Calvin declares, "When Christ is preached [made known to us] the Kingdom of Heaven is opened to us so that being raised from death we may live the life of God."[1] This is a life filled to overflowing with love, grace, beauty, peace, creativity. This is the life embodied in Jesus, the Christ. In the prologue to his gospel, John writes of Jesus:

> In the beginning was the Word, and the Word was with God, and the Word was God. He was with God in the beginning. Through him all things were made; without him nothing was made that has been made. In him was life, and that life was the light of all mankind . . . The Word became flesh and made his dwelling among us. We have seen his glory, the glory of the one and only Son, who came from the Father, full of grace and truth . . . Out of his fullness we have all received grace in place of grace already given. For the law was given through Moses; grace and truth came through Jesus Christ. No one has ever seen God, but the one and only Son, who is himself God and is in closest relationship with the Father, has made him known. (John 1:1–4, 14, 16–18)

These words strike me with the beauty of their ideal for our lives: "light," "grace," "truth." John proclaims that this life was embodied in Jesus. Further, when we enter into a relationship with Jesus as our Savior and Lord, we enter into this life that Jesus shares with God the Father/God the Mother and God the Spirit. The existential experience of this "eternal" life is joy.

This is the next great promise John makes in his letter: that a prime characteristic of the life we can share with God is joy:

> We proclaim to you what we have seen and heard, so that you also may have fellowship with us. And our fellowship is with the Father and with his Son, Jesus Christ. We write this to make our joy complete. (1:3–4)

1. Calvin, *Commentaries*, 160.

At first glance, this passage may not seem like a promise for us. Yet the British theologian John Stott sees in John's use of the pronoun *our*, the inclusion of both John and those to whom the letter is addressed.[2] In other words, it is joyful both to enter into this life of God and to see the readers of his letter enter into communion with the Father/the Mother and Son, as John has. Centuries before John wrote his letter, David proclaimed this same truth in song: "You [God] make known to me the path of life; you will fill me with joy in your presence, with eternal pleasures at your right hand" (Psalm 16:11).

This is good stuff. But do we really believe it? As Christians we profess that Jesus is the Way, the Truth, and the Life. Yet as we live out our lives, it sometimes looks a lot more like we believe that Oprah is the Way, Bill O'Reilly is the Truth, and Kim Kardashian is the Life. We tend to model our lives on those people we can observe in the world around us. And we can't observe Jesus in the same manner that we observe celebrities, newsmakers, or our neighbors.

In our congregation, we occasionally sing a hymn titled, "We Walk by Faith and Not by Sight." The lyrics acknowledge:

> We walk by faith and not by sight; No gracious words we hear from Christ, who spoke as none e'er spoke; but we believe Him near. / We may not touch His hands and side, nor follow where He trod; But in His promise we rejoice, And cry, "My Lord and God!"[3]

Yet even those of us who are not from Missouri tend toward the philosophy engraved on their license plates—we don't trust the sales pitch; we want someone to "Show me." Without a living body, one that we can see, touch, hear, smell (?!), or even just follow on Instagram, it can be extremely difficult to believe that Jesus existed, let alone that he is the Messiah.

John speaks directly to those doubts in the opening of this letter. He writes, "That which was from the beginning, which we

2. Stott, *Letters of John*, 69.
3. Alford, *Presbyterian Hymnal*, 399.

have *heard*, which we have *seen with our eyes*, which we have *looked* at and *our hands have touched*—this we proclaim concerning the Word of life. The life *appeared*; we have *seen* it and testify to it, and we proclaim to you the eternal life, which was with the Father and has *appeared* to us. We proclaim to you what we have *seen* and *heard*." Even those of us who are not too quick on the uptake, as I often am not, can catch John's emphasis (though the italics are mine). John seeks to assure us that he has personally encountered the risen Lord. The assertion of the church is that the gospels and the letters of the New Testament are based on firsthand accounts. Even if the writing wasn't always done by the witnesses themselves, the words were at least written by those who heard the stories from the witnesses directly.

Still, this makes the foundation of our beliefs fairly shaky. At best, our belief is third-hand. In fact, this is all so dicey that Jesus had to say an extra prayer for us. In John's gospel, Jesus prays not for his immediate disciples only but also for "those who will believe in me through their message" (John 17:20). That's us!

That said, we believe in the existence of a myriad of people for whom we have only secondhand or third-hand reports. For instance, I suspect that everyone reading this book believes that Julius Caesar existed. But why do we believe this? Personally, we have no more firsthand evidence to prove that the emperor JC existed than we do for the son of God JC. We simply trust that someone has done the research to establish the likelihood that the stories are true and that those who have taught us about Caesar believe this research to be credible. At that point, it is up to us to decide whether we think our teachers are credible. When put this way, it is a wonder we ever believe that anyone existed if we haven't met them personally.

John knew that many would doubt the stories they heard about Jesus or the impact he claimed Jesus could have on their lives. John knew that many would distrust his claim that Jesus could fill them with life and joy. So John does everything he can to assure those who read, or hear, his claims that he has experienced, firsthand, the life and joy that Christ brings. For John, this experience of life and joy has been so profound that he will not rest until others are brought into the same experience. He openly admits, "We proclaim to you what we have seen and heard, so that you also may have fellowship with us" (1:3).

In this passage from John, I prefer to translate the word "fellowship," from the Greek word *koinōnia*, as "communion." To me, *fellowship* brings to mind a gaggle of church folk wearing outdated clothes and talking over watery coffee in Styrofoam cups. *Communion* brings to mind the sacrament in which we take into our souls the flesh and blood of Jesus Christ. John is speaking of a relationship between persons, human and divine, that unites their very souls. John hopes that others will be drawn into the same experience of the life of God that he has experienced himself. When this happens, their joy and his, yours and mine, "our joy" will be complete.

Life and joy. Jesus offers more of both to anyone willing to believe in him. It would be great to hear it straight from his mouth, to touch his side and see the look in his eyes. We won't ever have that chance, but John did. And because he did, because he shared that experience with others, "the Kingdom of Heaven is opened to us so that being raised from death we may live the life of God."[4]

4. See note 1 above.

# Chapter Two

# The Light of the World

*This is the message we have heard from him and declare to you: God is light; in him there is no darkness at all. (1 John 1:5)*

I will readily admit that I am not the brightest bulb in the standard four-pack. In trying to grasp *big* concepts, especially, I find that I am often greatly helped with visual aids, whether of the literal or figurative kind. Thankfully, God has taken pity on folks like me and packed the pages of the Bible full of metaphors and similes—visual aids for the mind. A frequently cited example of this is God as "the *Rock* of our salvation." Now that is a weighty word; it's a good word to work with. A guy like me can go for a hike on Mount Rainier, see some spectacular boulder and begin to understand God a little more firmly.

Other examples of this figurative language abound in scripture: *eagle, shepherd, gate, bread.* Yet, John Stott proclaims, "Of the statements about the essential Being of God, none is more comprehensive than 'God is light."[1] Again, I make no claims to genius or scientific acumen, but even I find this image a fertile area for

1. Stott, *Letters of John*, 74–75.

exploration, particularly in the similar role light and Christ have in illumining the path of our lives.

Longtime Presbyterian pastor and author Earl Palmer helpfully reminds us that the biblical writer John was focusing on this aspect when he wrote, "God is light" (1:5). In his book on 1 John from the Communicator's Commentary series, Palmer notes, "What is important to remember in understanding what John means by light . . . is that his teaching is rooted more in the Old Testament understanding of light . . . than in the Greek philosophical understanding of th[is] concept . . . In the Old Testament, light has to do with *finding the path*."[2] In the early 1980s, Amy Grant popularized this Old Testament sense of light's function in a hit tune based on Psalm 119:105 (King James Version): "Thy word is a lamp unto my feet and a light unto my path." Even in the written-in-Greek New Testament, we read, "When Jesus spoke . . . to the people, he said, 'I am the light of the world. Whoever follows me will never walk in darkness, but will have the light of life" (John 8:12).

My wife can vouch for the importance of light in finding your way. When she was in high school, she and her family spent a week on the island of Maui. As many others have, they decided one day to climb to the top of Mt. Haleakala, the volcano that looms over the entire island. They had read that climbing the mountain very early in the day, so that they might view the sunrise from the volcano's rim, would be an experience they would never forget. That turned out to be true but not for the reason they had expected.

Rising early one morning, they drove up the mountain as far as the road would allow. They then hiked the rest of the way to the rim—in the dark. Figuring they had gone far enough, they stopped their trek, sat down, and waited. As the sun burst over the edge of the horizon, the array and depth of colors took their breath away, as did the other reality that the sun's rays revealed: they were sitting about three feet from the edge of a precipitous cliff! Had they continued their hike even a stride or two more, their darkened path might have led them to death. Until the sun

2. Palmer, *1, 2, 3 John*, 27.

rose and illuminated their path, they didn't have a clue where their path was leading.

It saddens me that many of us walk through much of our lives in a similar darkness. Often, we don't realize how dangerous our path is. Or how foolish. I live in the birthplace of Starbucks Coffee, and so I once took particular note of the story of a young man who made it his life's goal to visit every Starbucks outlet in the world. At that point he had racked up more than 271,000 miles on his Acura Integra, spending roughly five years of his life in this pursuit. He had visited more than 3,200 Starbucks stores in North America and 38 in the United Kingdom. As I read about his journey, I had the distinct feeling that one day the light may go on and he may come to realize that there are worthier pursuits in life. As I thought again about this young man a few years later, I searched for information on how far he had gotten. In an interview given in 2014, he made a partial concession, admitting, "I do not expect to ever complete the project, as I have every reason to think that Starbucks will outlive me." However, he continued, "But as long as there are new stores to visit, I will try to visit them . . . Pointless though it may be, a goal is a goal."[3]

As pointless as this young man's journey is, self-admittedly, it is no less enlightened than many of the paths we tread. Several years ago, a team of authors led by Robert N. Bellah presented a profoundly disturbing portrait of life in America titled *Habits of the Heart*. The book opens with a description of four typical Americans. The first life portrayed is that of a man they refer to as Brian. At the time of the sketch, Brian has already been through one marriage. He admits that he focused too much on his job, neglecting his family. So in his second marriage, Brian decides that this time his new wife and children will be his priority. Initially, his decision sounded to me like a sign of maturity. Then, I read further:

> Despite the personal triumph Brian's life represents, despite the fulfillment he seems to experience, there is still something uncertain, something poignantly unresolved

3. Binns, "Coffee fanatic admits defeat," *Metro*, May 19, 2014, http://metro.co.uk/.

about his story. The difficulty becomes evident when Brian tries to explain why it is that his current life is, in fact, better than his earlier life built around single-minded devotion to his career. His description of his reasons for changing his life and of his current happiness seems to come down mainly to a shift in his notions of what would make him happy. His new goal—devotion to marriage and children—seems as arbitrary and unexamined as his earlier pursuit of material success . . . Brian sees himself as consistently pursuing a utilitarian calculus— devotion to his own self-interest . . . For Brian . . . the goal of a good life is to achieve the priorities you have set for yourself. But how do you know that your present priorities are better than those of your past, or better than those of other people?[4]

In John's language, Brian continues to walk in darkness, of a sort.

It is important to emphasize that Bellah et al., cast Brian and the other three as types, meaning that the paths of their lives parallel the paths of a significant majority of the lives of people in the United States today. Truthfully, far too many of us blindly follow our family, friends, and idols into deeper darkness, and at the same time, we lead others, those who foolishly think we know the way to enlightenment, on this same dark path behind us.

Yet, into that darkness Jesus comes along side us—the Brians, the Starbucks überfans, me and you—and says, "I am the light of the world. Whoever follows me will never walk in darkness, but will have the light of life." Jesus offers us a truly enlightened understanding of the "nature of success, the meaning of freedom and the requirements of justice."[5] In the light of Christ we see goodness, beauty, truth. As Palmer puts it, "When Jesus Christ is Lord of our life, then we see the road more clearly. Jesus Christ not only shows us who the Father is, He also shows us who we are and where we are."[6]

4. Bellah et al., *Habits of the Heart*, 5–6, 21.
5. Ibid, 21.
6. Palmer, *1, 2, 3 John*, 28.

# The Light of the World

We are lost without the light of Christ in our lives, yet even with this light we will not understand, know, or see everything. In the physical realm, visible light amounts to only one-thousandth of the electromagnetic spectrum. In the spiritual realm, much remains shrouded for us, perhaps to a similar degree. Yet the light of Christ in our lives still leads us toward the fullness of beauty, goodness, truth, health, joy, peace, and love.

In addition, Christ's disciples are invited to play a role in lighting the way toward this fullness of life for others by reflecting Christ's light in the world. Jesus privileges his followers with the affirmation, "You are the light of the world" (Matthew 5:14). While studying how light works in general, I stumbled upon an analogy in addition to "reflection" that helped me understand how we might embody this light of Christ.

Reflection is the more commonly understood process which we experience regularly, seeing light rays bounce off of mirrors or other smooth surfaces especially. Refraction was a process with which I was less familiar. So, I did what all neophytes to a subject do these days: I googled it. The website science.howstuffworks. com defines *refraction* in the following way:

> Refraction occurs when a ray of light passes from one transparent medium (air, let's say) to a second transparent medium (water). When this happens, light changes speed and the light ray bends . . . The amount of bending, or angle of refraction, of the light wave depends on how much the material slows down the light. Diamonds wouldn't be so glittery if they didn't slow down incoming light much more than, say, water does. Diamonds have a higher index of refraction than water, which is to say that those sparkly, costly light traps slow down light to a greater degree.[7]

Ideally, the lives of the followers of Christ anthropomorphize this process of refraction. The scriptures frequently encourage disciples to "dwell in" God and allow God to dwell in them, to "abide in" God and allow God to abide in them. This all takes time

7. Freudenrich and Harris, "How Light Works," Refraction.

(and often a lot of quiet too). After a while, however, the light of God begins to shine from within. These lives begin to shine like diamonds refracting light. Christ has been allowed to dwell deep within them. In consequence, Christ shines out from them and yet their lives are authentically their own. The brilliance these diamond-lives reflect often draws attention from those longing to know the source of light, thereby pointing them in the direction of the true light of life, Christ Jesus.

In the closing stanza of her poem "St. Thomas Didymus,"[8] the late poet Denise Levertov brilliantly conveys the experience that communion with Jesus Christ can bring to all our lives. Recounting the moment when St. Thomas reaches out to touch the wound in the side of the risen Lord, Levertov imagines St. Thomas' experience as one not of "shame" but "light. Light streaming into me, over me, filling the room." Within this light of Christ, St. Thomas experiences "all things quicken to color, to form." Ultimately, St. Thomas becomes aware of "a vast unfolding design lit by the risen sun." I believe Levertov captures the essence of the experience we all will have the more we let the presence of Christ dwell in us, the longer we let the light of God abide in us.

Without the light of Christ in our lives we stumble about in darkness. We can't see beyond ourselves and offer little help to others. With the light of Christ in our lives we can see the way to the life of God. We can see the reality of the world all around us; and our lives become like diamonds reflecting the light of life to others.

8. Levertov, *Stream & Sapphire*, 84.

# Chapter Three

# Fess Up

*If we claim to have fellowship with him and yet walk in the darkness, we lie and do not live out the truth. But if we walk in the light, as he is in the light, we have fellowship with one another, and the blood of Jesus, his Son, purifies us from all sin. If we claim to be without sin, we deceive ourselves and the truth is not in us. If we confess our sins, he is faithful and just and will forgive us our sins and purify us from all unrighteousness. If we claim we have not sinned, we make him out to be a liar and his word is not in us. (1 John 1:6–10)*

One of the more delightful moments I experienced as a parent was watching my kids first learn the concept of hiding. They'd cover their eyes with their hands or put a blanket over their head, and I knew what they were thinking, "Wow, it's dark! I can't see anyone. That means they can't see me." They would triumphantly proclaim, "Can't see me!" Of course, I'd laugh because I did see them, they were sitting right there in front of me. They may have had a blanket covering their heads, but they hadn't vanished. As they grew older, at some point it dawned on them that they weren't tricking me. They had been visible the whole time. That's when they moved on to hide and seek.

Many of us adults try to play similar games with God. We try to cover up those actions of ours that have hurt others or that have caused us shame. We try to put some sort of blanket over them, to keep them secret. We keep them in the dark, and we think to ourselves, "I can't see God, so maybe God doesn't see these things." In John's letter, he has a pretty stark reminder that the joke is on us. In 1:8, John writes, "If we claim to be without sin, we deceive ourselves and the truth is not in us." One of the early leaders of the church, St. Augustine, echoed the words of John in the fourth century when he wrote, "The abyss of the human conscience lies naked to your eyes, O Lord, so would anything in me be secret even if I were unwilling to confess to you? I would be hiding you from myself, but not myself from you."[1] Both Augustine and John profess the same harsh truth: nothing is hidden from God.

One of the most haunting professions of this reality comes in Psalm 139. The psalmist writes,

> You have searched me, Lord, and you know me. You know when I sit down and when I rise, you perceive my thoughts from afar, you discern my going out and my lying down, you are familiar with all my ways. Before a word is on my tongue you, Lord, know it completely. You hem me in behind and before, and you lay your hand upon me. Such knowledge is too wonderful for me, too lofty for me to attain. Where can I go from your Spirit? Where can I flee from your presence? If I go up to the heavens, you are there; if I make my bed in the depths, you are there. If I rise on the wings of the dawn, if I settle on the far side of the sea, even there your hand will guide me, your right hand will hold me fast. If I say, "Surely the darkness will hide me and the light become night around me," even the darkness will not be dark to you; the night will shine like the day, for darkness is as light to you. For you created my inmost being; you knit me together in my mother's womb. (vv. 1–13)

This psalm always disturbs me. Is it good news or bad news that God is with us *everywhere*? That nothing is hidden from God?

1. Augustine, *Confessions*, 197.

Furthermore, when we claim to be without sin, not only do we deceive ourselves, but as John warns us in 1:10, "If we claim we have not sinned, we make [God] out to be a liar." We make God out to be a liar because, over and over again, the Scriptures proclaim, in God's name, "*All* have sinned and fall short of the glory of God." The italics are mine, but the words are Paul's, from Romans. There is no equivocation—all of us have sinned. To say otherwise is not true, to say that we have not sinned is to put a blanket over our own heads and to insult God.

Thanks be to God, John has more to say on the subject. In 1:9, he adds, "If we confess our sins, [God] is faithful and just and will forgive us our sins and purify us from all unrighteousness." For many of us, the idea of confession fills the mind with visions of a dimly lit, darkly stained wooden booth, a latticework separating us and our crimes from a somber and humorless priest. Yet in John's Greek, the word *confess* has a much more interesting connotation. In the Greek the word is *homologeō*, which literally means "to agree with someone" or "to say in a like manner." The Rev. Earl Palmer expands our understanding of what John may be conveying: "We are told by John that our responsibility is to agree with God about the nature of our crises."[2] To admit it.

John writes a great deal about walking in the light. Palmer ties these two ideas together: "To walk in the light does not mean that a human being is sinless and flawless; rather to walk in the light means that a human being as a sinner is, in the light, fully aware that he or she is a sinner."[3] "To walk in the light" means to be aware of our fallen nature, our brokenness. "To walk in the light" means to see ourselves for who we really are. Rather than being fearful of the result of such honesty, John emboldens us with the promise of a wonderful outcome. In 1:9, he counters our suspicious inclination with the proclamation, "If we confess our sins, God is faithful and just and will forgive us our sins."

*Forgive* is another one of those words that can lose important nuances when translated from the original. The Greek word behind

2. Palmer, *1, 2, 3 John*, 31–32.
3. Ibid, 31.

this translation, *aphē*, literally means "to leave behind." In our lives when we sin, when we make a mistake—knowingly or not—when we do something we shouldn't do or don't do something we should do, it burdens our soul. Like the chain that bound Jacob Marley in Charles Dickens's *A Christmas Carol*, every sin becomes another link that binds us and weighs us down. But God breaks the chain that burdens our souls. God breaks it, leaves it behind, and frees us to become the people who God intended us to be.

One of the most powerful images of leaving our sins behind us that I know of is seen in the movie *The Mission*. Robert DeNiro plays a seventeenth-century Spanish mercenary and slave trader named Roberto Mendoza. In addition to a grizzly scene where Mendoza captures human beings in a net like one might catch a wild animal, we witness this slave trader murder his own brother in a fit of jealous rage. Overcome by horror and sorrow, Mendoza attempts to keep himself from facing the full consequences of his actions by holing up in a mission for six months and speaking to no one. Finally, confronted by a priest portrayed by Jeremy Irons, Mendoza is challenged to contend with his sinfulness head-on. The now remorseful conquistador packs all the accoutrements of his previous life—his armor, his swords and knives, his helmet, his elaborate attire—into one gigantic bundle. The priest ropes this massive burden to Mendoza's upper body and leads him on an arduous journey that lasts for days. They wade across swift flowing rivers and along muddy trails through dense jungle. All the while, this poor, repentant man continues to drag his massive burden behind him. The weight and awkwardness of this gigantic bundle causes him to struggle for nearly every step. It trails in the dirt, catches branches, wedges between rocks. By the time they reach their destination above a tremendous waterfall—the destination being a village of the very tribe that Mendoza used to enslave—Mendoza lies face down flat on the dirt, broken and utterly exhausted. In the penultimate moment, one of the men from the village, having recognized his people's former tormentor, grabs a knife, pulls Mendoza's head from the dirt and places the knife at his throat. Mendoza offers no resistance. The villager exchanges a few words with the priest; and then begins to cut the rope from Mendoza's back. With a few strokes of the knife, the villager cuts Mendoza free and pushes the enormous bundle off the cliff into the river that carries it away. Finally, completely relieved of all his shame and guilt, this forgiven man sobs and sobs and sobs overcome with sheer joy. This is the release we receive from God through the life, death, and resurrection of Jesus, the Christ. The writer of Psalm 103 gives us another profound and beautiful image of this grace of God: "As far as the east is from the west, so far has God removed our transgressions from us" (v. 12). When God forgives us, our sins are truly removed from us.

Delightfully, the forgiveness of sins, their removal from our lives, is not even the end of God's grace. The second part of John's proclamation in 1:9 promises another profound benefit from confessing our sins. John writes, "If we confess our sins, he is faithful and just, and will forgive our sins *and* purify us from all unrighteousness." Again, the italics are mine to emphasize this glorious two-for-one deal.

Since I am about to make another Greek-to-English translation point, I must say that in this chapter, I'm beginning to feel a bit like the dad in the movie *My Big Fat Greek Wedding* who believed that all words originate from Greek. While not true of all words, I do know that our English word *catharsis* comes from the Greek root word *katharizō*. It is this word that John wrote when he was trying to convey what God's grace does for us when we confess our sins. Catharsis—to clean out, to purge, to get rid of all the yuck! When we confess our sins, God cleans us out, God purges us of our sin, God gets rid of all the yuck. And the effects can be astonishing! We lose anxiety, we lose fear, we lose guilt. Sometimes our lives may even become healthier physically. Plenty of research has shown that unburdening ourselves of psychological guilt can often bring physical healing and health. In Psalm 32, the writer declares, "When I kept silent, my bones wasted away through my groaning all day long . . . Then I acknowledged my sin to you and didn't cover up my iniquity" (vv. 3, 5). Joy and restoration followed.

In this part of his letter, John alludes to another positive effect confession can have on our lives; but one that may not be as immediately connected in our minds. In an earlier verse, 1:7, John promises, "If we walk in the light [by confessing our sins], as [God] is in the light, we have fellowship with one another." Earl Palmer helps us see how confession and community go hand in hand when he writes, "John teaches us that the openness before God that enables our forgiveness also enables our fellowship. Fellowship is not founded upon deception and never has been."[4] The more we share openly the fullness of our hearts and minds with those close to us, the stronger our communion will be with one another and with God.

Considering all of these profoundly positive effects that come from confessing our sins—forgiveness, cleansing, communion— you'd think we'd want to confess so often that there would be a line at every available confessional booth. Yet, from my experience, even those of us who know the promises made to us rarely take the time to acknowledge and confess the worst in us. I believe that the impediment of fear often bars the door to a robust confessional life. Because those who have risked vulnerability within the church, those who have confessed what they've done and revealed their most intimate battles, have often been hurt by others using their defenselessness to hurt them, we're afraid of what our neighbor might do with our confession. We may even be afraid ourselves of what we might find if we take the time to examine the darkest corners of our hearts. Further, as much as we've heard, read, and experienced otherwise, I think many of us are still afraid that if God knows what we have done, what we have conceived of in our hearts and minds, God will punish us. We can't let go of the suspicion that God won't love us anymore if God knows the full truth. We forget that, as John reminds us, God provides a faithful and just ear for our confessions. We forget that God's justice includes forgiveness, not lightning bolts from the sky, because Christ's sacrifice has already covered any price to be paid. As we read in 1:7, "If we walk in the light, as he is in the light, we have fellowship with

4. Palmer, *1, 2, 3 John*, 32.

one another, and [literally, it should be translated—*as*] the blood of Jesus . . . purifies us from all sin."

My all-time favorite passage of Scripture (*not* because I learned of it from seeing it on a placard in the background of countless NFL broadcast crowd shots but because it so perfectly reveals the heart of God), John 3:16–17, proclaims:

> For God so loved the world that he gave his one and only Son, that whoever believes in him shall not perish but have eternal life. For God did not send his son into the world to condemn the world, but to save the world through him.

Through Christ, we are justified before God. We can boldly enter into God's presence. We don't have to fear punishment. God's love for us, for all of us, prompted this reconciliation. Some people falsely claim that God's wrath was the reason for Christ's coming, but the Scriptures remind us that God initiated our salvation out of love for us.

Many of those who knew God truly recognized God's grace even before Jesus arrived on the planet. Again, the writer of Psalm 103 bursts forth, "Praise the Lord, my soul; all my inmost being, praise his holy name . . . and forget not his benefits—who forgives all your sins and heals all your diseases, who redeems your life from the pit and crowns you with love and compassion" (vv. 1–4). Just a little further on the Psalmist continues:

> The Lord is compassionate and gracious, slow to anger, abounding in love . . . he does not treat us as our sins deserve or repay us according to our iniquities. For as high as the heavens are above the earth, so great is his love for those who fear him . . . As a Father has compassion on his children, so the Lord has compassion on those who fear him. (vv. 8, 10–11, 13)

And I love the next line, "For he remembers that we are dust" (v. 14). God knows who we are. God knows everything we've done. We're the ones with the blanket over our heads when we don't confess our sins, when we don't admit them.

The good news is that we don't even have to try to hide. God loves us no matter what we have done. God loves us even if flood lights were to reveal our ugliest acts, thoughts, and fantasies. Earl Palmer writes: "There is no cause for the acceleration of joy that can match the shock of recognition that I am loved for who I really am."[5] I believe we may not ever be able to hear enough of John proclaiming, "If we walk in the light as he is in the light we have fellowship with one another as the blood of Jesus his son purifies us from all sin." *All* sin. Full stop. God's forgiveness and cleansing and community and love is with us. God's love, as seen in the actions of Christ, should motivate us to step into the light and confess who we really are. God already knows everything; Jesus knew it when he gave his life for us. And now God stands with open arms and says, "Let me love you. Let me love you into wholeness." As human beings we have a need to confess, to admit before God, who we really have been, in order that we might become who we really are.

5. Palmer, *1, 2, 3 John*, 33.

| | |
|---|---|
| Title | Abide In Me: Being Fully Alive In Christ |
| Condition | Good |
| Location | Walden  Aisle G  Bay 06 Item 7654 |
| Description | May have some shelf-wear due to normal use. |
| Source | Prescanned |
| SKU | 0KVOV9002HX7 |
| ASIN | 1498291112 |
| Code | 9781498291118 |
| Employee | 1cstewardd |
| Date Added | 12/5/2021 9:23:19 AM |

## Chapter Four

# Hope is a Person

*My dear children, I write this to you so that you will not sin. But if anybody does sin, we have an advocate with the Father—Jesus Christ, the Righteous One. He is the atoning sacrifice for our sins, and not only for ours but also for the sins of the whole world. (1 John 2:1–2)*

Every week, millions of people gather in buildings of various sizes and shapes; sit on uncomfortable pews, benches, or seats; and perform elaborate rituals, some with props or bits of food. Every day of every week of every year, billions of people bend their knees, bow their heads, clasp their hands, close their eyes, and mutter words of varying formality and informality to an invisible noun, to a person, place, or thing that they cannot see. What is it that motivates so many of us to participate in religious ceremonies and rituals?

Almost all of the prominent religions in the world acknowledge the existence of a singular God or a variety of gods who either control life as we know it or who at least have a significant influence on our experience of the world. The hope of the followers who belong to these religions seems to be that they will enter into a relationship with God, or the gods, such that life will be peaceful, even joyful. Indeed, William Barclay, a Scottish pastor and a biblical scholar from the middle of last century, once asserted, "The great aim of all religion is fellowship with God, to know him as friend and to enter with joy and not fear, into his presence."[1]

This longing to find peace with the forces of the world, the forces in our lives, is a longing shared by even those who profess no religion. Whether it's a baseball player who superstitiously steps over a chalk line or a consumer who chooses to buy organic produce, almost everyone desires to be right with the world, to have a sense that we are not only not fighting against forces that may harm us but that we are living well. Ultimately, this longing leads most of the people in the world to some sort of belief in a metaphysical power and leads most of us to some form of organized religion. Though the attempt at satisfaction manifests in varying ways, it seems as though the saying from St. Augustine is universally true, "We have been made for Thee, O God, and our hearts will find no rest until they find their rest in Thee."

A thought from Barclay extends this idea that our hearts will find no rest until they find their rest in God: "It therefore follows that the supreme problem of religion is sin, for it is sin that interrupts fellowship with God."[2] It might be more appropriately stated that sin is not so much the supreme problem *of* religion but the supreme problem *for* religion to address—sin in this case being whatever separates us from God, whatever prevents us from finding our rest in the divine. Further, what most of us find when we examine scriptures or our own lives is that we, ourselves, are the ones who create that tumult and distance. It is our own thoughts, words, and deeds that lead us away from God. We are responsible for our sins. Whether we have done something extreme—like committed murder, something that everyone can look at and say, "Yeah, I can see how that separates us from God, who created life"—or whether, as Jesus says, we *merely* think of our neighbor or coworker in a degrading fashion, a neighbor or coworker who was created in God's image, these are things that increase the distance between us and God.

1. Barclay, *Letters of John*, 39.
2. Ibid.

With this in mind, we can understand the great attraction that religion holds for most of us: the world's biggest religions, at least as they are popularly practiced, give us something to *do* about sin. Light a candle, burn a stick of incense, say a rote prayer, donate money, sponsor a starving child in Africa, eat a chunk of bread, and wash it back with wine, and all will be right between us and God. The way we practice Christianity includes as many of these acts as any other major religion. And, if truth be told, most of us participate in these acts with the hope that our rote actions will eliminate the separation between ourselves and God.

Unfortunately, it doesn't work like that, at least according to the Christian Scriptures. Performing these acts of meditation, contrition, or service does not eliminate the separation. Our best efforts fall short—we simply can't keep up with the pace of our own sinning! And even when we feel somewhat on top of things, our acts don't relieve us entirely of our awareness that something is not right. When we try to expunge our sins by means of our own actions, we often find ourselves frustrated. We have failed to bridge the gap and we may even find ourselves *farther* from God.

But our hope does not lie in redoubling our efforts, in finding some new practice, discipline, or religion. Our hope is not in ourselves in any way. Our hope is in another person entirely; our hope is in Jesus Christ. John addresses this in his letter: "My dear children, I write this to you so that you will not sin. But if anybody does sin, we have an advocate with the Father—Jesus Christ, the Righteous One." (2:1) John is writing this to believers. John knows that we are going to sin, so he directs our attention to Jesus, our only hope. In more stark terms, John writes, "He is the atoning sacrifice for our sin" (2:2). As if that were not enough John goes on to make an assertion of truly epic proportions. John contends that Jesus is the atoning sacrifice not only for the sins of those who believe but also "the atoning sacrifice . . . for the sins of the whole world." The NIV adds no exclamation point, but I believe that one would certainly be appropriate, if not several. The hope of the world for eliminating the separation between human beings and

God is not in our own actions; our hope is not in ourselves. Our hope is in the person of Jesus Christ.

To further establish the unique role and work of Jesus in reconciling all persons to God, when John makes this proclamation he identifies Jesus in a more elaborate way than he typically does. John writes that our hope is in, specifically, "Jesus Christ, the Righteous One!" Each of these names that John uses reveals important aspects of Jesus' character and his role in our lives. For starters, John calls our savior "Jesus." He is Yeshua (an approximation of his name in Hebrew), a guy from a little town in the Middle East, Nazareth. Our hope rests with a person who, as a human, knows our human condition. As the writer of the book of Hebrews puts it:

> Both the one who makes people holy [Jesus] and those who are made holy [us] are of the same family . . . Since the children have flesh and blood, he too shared in their humanity so that by his death he might break the power of him who holds the power of death—that is, the devil . . . For this reason he had to be made like them, fully human in every way, in order that he might become a merciful and faithful high priest in service to God, and that he might make atonement for the sins of the people. Because he himself suffered when he was tempted, he is able to help those who are being tempted. (2:11, 14, 17–18)

John also calls Jesus "Christ," which is, essentially, the Greek translation of the Hebrew title "Messiah." This is a title given to the person God had promised to God's people; it literally means the "Anointed One" who serves as a mediator between us and God the Father/the Mother, our Creator. Jesus, the Christ, frees us from our slavery to sin and leads us into the kingdom of God.

John also adds the designation "the Righteous One." Notice the definite article. Jesus is not *a* righteous one; to his followers Jesus is *the* Righteous One. As followers of Christ we believe that Jesus is the only one to live a life in perfect communion with, and obedience to, God. Jesus fulfills that role as the only human who has lived an entirely sinless life; and, because Jesus is without sin, he is the only one holy enough to stand before God. That's what Jesus Christ the Righteous One does: he stands before God and, John tells us, speaks to God in our defense.

As the NIV does, some translations of this portion of John's letter even use the word "advocate" to describe Jesus. The role Jesus fills does have a legal sense to it. We have Jesus, the Christ, the Righteous One, God's own Son, defending our case; and, whatever one's view of divine justice, Jesus keeps us from suffering the worst of it. Lest we get too carefree with this get-out-of-jail-free card, however, John Stott elucidates a significant difference between what a normal defense attorney does and what Jesus does for us: "Our Advocate does not plead that we are innocent or adduce extenuating circumstances. He acknowledges our guilt and presents His vicarious work as the ground for our acquittal."[3]

At this point in John's letter many commentators start to wander into a bramble, a place where two paths diverge from the main path, winding through a thicket in opposite directions. Exactly *how* Jesus's "vicarious work" saves us has been the source of much spilt ink. Down one path are those who assert that Jesus *expiates* our sins. Expiation refers to an action that atones for an offence, a "covering over" or "blotting out" that makes the sin go away. Expiation is directed toward the action that caused the separation. Down the other path are those who assert that Jesus *propitiates* God's anger and wrath for our sin. Propitiation is directed toward God's response, or potential response, to a sinful action. Through propitiation, God's wrath is turned away from us and God is reconciled to us. On the one hand, those who espouse the idea of expiation tend to focus on God's love as Christ's motivation for his sacrificial act—God loves us too much to be angry about all this stuff, they might say, and so he just gets rid of the sin. On the other hand, those who espouse the idea of propitiation tend to focus on God's holiness as Christ's motivation—they might say that God hates sin so much that he cannot look past it; punishment must be doled out. According to this view, Jesus takes the punishment for all of us.

3. Stott, *Letters of John*, 86.

In trying to understand for myself what John may have meant with his choice of the word *hilasmos,* which the NIV translates as "atoning sacrifice," I consulted the seminarian's bible for Greek word meanings in the New Testament, the BAGD.[4] Those initials stand for Bauer, Arndt, Gingrich, and Danker, the gentlemen who produced the august reference book *A Greek-English Lexicon of the New Testament and Other Early Christian Literature.* It's the definitive source for narrowing down the original meanings of words in the Greek Scriptures. I was hoping the BAGD would tell me which interpretation best captured the original understanding, propitiation or expiation. In the veritable wisdom of Bauer, Arndt, Gingrich and Danker, they listed both meanings, propitiation and expiation. I believe they got it right. It seems to me that Christ's act of self-giving on the cross accomplishes both aspects. Jesus' act of self-giving on the cross reveals both God's love and God's holiness. This two-sided coin was earlier proclaimed by another of God's children in Psalm 85:

> You, Lord, showed favor to your land; you restored the fortunes of Jacob. You forgave the iniquity of your people and covered all their sins [expiation]. You set aside all your wrath and turned from your fierce anger [propitiation]. (vv.1–3)

God's holiness seemingly demands propitiation; God's grace seemingly demands expiation. The death of God's Son provides both.

Ultimately, though, the question of *how* this all works is less important than the question of *who* accomplished it. In John 1:29, he records the following scene: "The next day John [the Baptist] saw Jesus coming toward him and said, 'Look, the Lamb of God, who takes away the sin of the world!'" John the Baptist doesn't explain how; he points to whom. The belief of those who follow Jesus as both Savior and Lord is that both the Old Testament and the New point to Jesus Christ as the one who leads all people to God, who Jesus and the Apostle's called "Father." As Barclay reminded

---

4. Bauer et al., *Greek-English Lexicon,* s.v. "hilasterion."

us earlier, sin is the "supreme problem" religion must resolve, "for sin . . . interrupts fellowship with God." Therefore, Jesus is the supreme answer of religion, for Jesus restores our communion with God. As John puts it, "[W]e have an advocate with the Father—Jesus Christ, the Righteous One. He is the atoning sacrifice for our sins, and not only for ours but also for the sins of the whole world" (2:1–2) Jesus is not only our hope but the hope of the world.

I forget this too often. While trying to be a Christian I forget Christ. A while back, Nike had a television ad that showed a typical, middle-aged guy heading out for a jog. As he casually runs down a quiet, tree-lined street, another runner pops out from behind some bushes and starts running alongside the original guy. Soon, more and more runners join the pair and the pace picks up dramatically. The original runner keeps looking over his shoulder at the growing hoard, trying to outrun them all. As he finally gets back to his house, runs up the steps, and slams the door behind him, the ad closes with the tag line "What are you training for?"

This is a great question for Christians to adapt to our lives of discipleship. What are we doing all this Christian stuff for? Why do we gather in buildings of various sizes and shapes; sit on uncomfortable pews or seats; and perform elaborate rituals? Why do we bend our knees, bow our heads, and mutter words in prayer? Why do we give our money and our time? Are we running from forces we fear may do us harm, or are we running because God has blessed us with life? Are we doing these things to earn communion with God, or do we do these things because of our communion with God?

Our hope in life, and death, is not in what we do but in Jesus Christ and what he has already done for us. Our sin separates us from communion with God, but John declares that Jesus eliminates that separation. John Calvin also assures us, "We contract new guilt daily, and yet there is a remedy for reconciling us to God, if we flee to Christ; and this is alone that in which consciences can acquiesce, in which is included the righteousness of man, in which is founded the hope of salvation."[5] Hope is a person. And

5. Calvin, *Commentaries*, 170–171.

salvation is a relationship with that person, with Jesus Christ, the Righteous One.

# Chapter Five

# Let It Be

*As for you, see that what you have heard from the beginning remains in you. If it does, you also will remain in the Son and in the Father. And this is what he promised us—eternal life (1 John 2:24–25)*

I've been at this discipleship thing for more than thirty years now: attempting to follow Christ, reading the Bible, worshipping in various congregations, praying. Still, I occasionally puzzle over whether or not I am really being transformed and living the life God would have me live. In the first flush years of discipleship, the contrast between *before* Jesus and *after* Jesus was so drastic that no doubt entered my mind. However, once that first blush faded, I began to take a closer look in the mirror, and I found that I recognized far too much of my old self.

For all of us who ever wonder whether we are headed in the right direction, John provides us with a remarkably simple test. In 1 John, he writes the following:

> We know that we have come to know him if we keep his commands. Whoever says, "I know him," but does not do what he commands is a liar, and the truth is not in that person. But if anyone obeys his word, love for God is truly made complete in them. This is how we know we

are in him: Whoever claims to live in him must live as
Jesus did. (2:3–6)

Do we want to know how we are doing as Jesus' disciples? If
we are obeying his commands, John says we're doing well; if we
aren't obeying those commands, it might be time to worry.

I bet I am not the only one who begins to shift in my seat
when the matter gets stated as plainly as John states it. Many of Jesus' commands are tremendously (enlarge the font, put it in bold,
add an exclamation point) difficult to obey. And in case that was
not enough to make us scoot forward and take note, John thwacks
us again:

> Anyone who claims to be in the light but hates a brother
> or sister is still in the darkness. Anyone who loves their
> brother and sister lives in the light, and there is nothing
> in them to make them stumble. But anyone who hates a
> brother or sister is in the darkness and walks around in
> the darkness. They do not know where they are going,
> because the darkness has blinded them. (2:9–11)

I can almost hear John's readers and fellow Christians inter-
rupting him at this point—"Hold up there, buddy, now you're getting personal." Of course, that's the point. It is personal.

As an example, I have often been asked into arguments, in
Christian circles, about the respective roles of spouses in marriage.
Usually, one of the two debaters is brandishing Paul's words in
Ephesians and trying to tell the other one what their role is (and
how to do it better). No matter who is trying to get the upper hand,
my response is always the same: "What do the Scriptures say *your*
role is?" I then make the following suggestion: "When you feel
that you are fulfilling your role 100 percent, come back and we'll
talk about how the other spouse is doing." Silence usually follows.
When we honestly assess our own actions, we often find that our
obedience is lacking. None of us obeys all of Christ's commands
all the time.

Most of us are well-intentioned sinners, and so we respond to marital advice or words like John's by buckling down and trying even harder. We add regiments of meditation, contrition, and service, like I described in the previous chapter, and double down on being good. One of the most earnest practitioners of this approach of which I know was Benjamin Franklin. At one point in his adult life, Franklin committed himself to systematically eradicating bad behavior and bad thoughts from his personality. To do so, he kept a detailed daily journal in which he logged every sin in a wide variety of categories. As he noticed the accumulation of sins within a specific category, he would focus on that category until he felt he had it under control. Eventually, he thought, he would be able to conquer each category and become a completely virtuous human being. He never made it. In fact, Franklin realized that even if he had managed to clear all his columns of bad marks, he would likely feel too proud of his accomplishment: "Even if I could conceive that I had completely overcome [pride], I should probably be proud of my humility."[1] He realized that sinless obedience was impossible.

This is also familiar territory for a more contemporary American, Larry Crabb. A well-known author within Christian circles, Crabb has been a psychotherapist for more than twenty-five years. In his insightful book *Connections*, Crabb makes a very startling admission:

> For the most part, I've been a 'figure-things-out-expose-what's-wrong-then-make-appropriate-corrections' type of counselor. Give me a problem, and I go to work. Panic attacks? I'll help you find the deeper fears you've never faced and work them through. Addiction problems? It may take a while, but I'll root out your idolatrous demand for reliable pleasure and your hatred for an unmanageable God, then I'll guide you on a journey through terrified self-dependence toward vigorous trust. When it's time, I'll throw in a healthy dash of instruction, some generous tablespoons of advice and exhortation, then I'll let things simmer for a while under my

1. Franklin, *Autobiography*, 72.

watchful eye of accountability. Like most counselors, churches, and families, I depend on the tried-and-true approaches of fix-what's-wrong and do-what's-right to promote good change in others. But the result has not always been what I'd hoped for, either in myself or others . . . I want a life of soaring on wings like eagles, running along with renewed strength, and walking through deep valleys without growing faint [Isaiah 40:31] for my wife, my two sons, my two daughters-in-law, my friends, my clients, myself. [But] I'm convinced I won't help you or me get there by merely understanding problems . . . or exhorting worthy change.[2]

We can't do this on our own. In fact, this task proves so exhausting that many people give up the effort. John notes in his letter, particularly the second chapter, that there are a number of people in the community who have essentially stopped trying:

Dear children, this is the last hour; and as you have heard that the antichrist is coming, even now many antichrists have come. This is how we know it is the last hour. They went out from us, but they did not really belong to us. For if they had belonged to us, they would have remained with us; but their going showed that none of them belonged to us. (2:18–19)

John is writing this letter to the community that is still hanging on. He is writing to warn his fellow Christians not to be like those who have given up. Specifically, he says, "I am writing these things to you about those who are trying to lead you astray" (v. 26).

Yet to avoid being led astray—or, stated positively, to live the life that God is calling us to live—John does not say, "Let's take a look at why we are tempted." He does not write, "Just say, 'NO!'" Rather, John refers to one of the most important existential truths we need to be aware of in order to live the life into which God invites us. John writes, "As for you, the anointing you received from [Christ] remains in you, and you do not need anyone to teach you

2. Crabb, *Connecting*, 8–9.

... his anointing teaches you about all things and ... that anointing is real" (v. 27).

Although he uses different language to express his thought, Larry Crabb reaches the same conclusion that John came to after trying to promote change in his own way for over two decades. As Crabb writes:

> It's become clear to me ... that God handles things a bit differently. He does, of course, rebuke and exhort, and his Spirit does search our hearts for hidden matters that interfere with trust. *But the absolute center of what he does to help us change is to reveal himself to us, to give us a taste of what he's really like, and to pour his life into us.*[3]

The italics are Crabb's, but if he hadn't included them I would have. His emphasis brings out the vital point I believe we must understand. God's anointing of us, the pouring of his life into us, brings about any worthwhile change in our lives.

Both Crabb and John emphasize the necessity of openly confronting and acknowledging our sinfulness. John articulates this using the vocabulary of darkness and light, exhorting us to "walk in the light," to be honest about our failings. This is an important aspect of a trusting relationship with God in Christ.

However, it is not a given that we will follow this bright path. There are many who walk in the shadows cast by the "world," John's catchall word for things that are the antithesis of God. In 2:16, he cites three marks of those who follow these "worldly" ways: "For everything in the world—the lust of the flesh, the lust of the eyes, and the pride of life—comes not from the Father but from the world." If achieving these marks—lust and pride—resulted in winning the lottery, I'd be a rich man. Then again, I'd have to split the pot with most of my friends and neighbors, who I suspect have also achieved these "winning" marks.

Rather than give up on us all, John reminds those of us who have experienced the presence of Christ that there is yet a significant power that lies within us: "But you have an anointing from the

3. Ibid, 9.

Holy One . . . the anointing you received from him remains in you" (vv. 20, 27). I hold the same belief as Barclay, who believed that the "anointing" to which John refers is at least in part the Holy Spirit.[4] The prophet Ezekiel predicted no less, centuries before John was even alive:

> Then the nations will know that I am the Lord, declares the Sovereign Lord, when I am proved holy through you before their eyes . . . I will sprinkle clean water on you, and you will be clean . . . I will give you a new heart and put a new spirit in you; I will remove from you your heart of stone and give you a heart of flesh. And I will put my Spirit in you and move you to follow my decrees, and be careful to keep my laws. (36:23, 25–27)

Jesus, himself, promised his disciples:

> If you love me, keep my commands. And I will ask the Father, and he will give you another advocate to help you and be with you forever—the Spirit of truth. The world cannot accept him, because it neither sees him nor knows him. But you know him, for he lives with you and will be in you . . . when he, the Spirit of truth, comes, he will guide you into all truth. (John 14:15–17; 16:12–13)

The historical event of Pentecost, recorded in the book of Acts, realized these prophecies when the Holy Spirit filled the disciples of Christ.

The Spirit of Christ is alive within us, at work inside us. Crabb explains what this means for us:

> At the exact center of the human personality is a capacity to give and receive in relationship, a capacity or possibility that defines what it means to be alive as a human being. When that capacity is corrupted, when, rather than giving who we are and receiving others for who they are, we use others to gain what we think we need and to protect ourselves from the harm others can inflict on us, then we are dead. We are sub-human. We give evidence that we have fallen to a level lower than our intended

---

4. Barclay, *Letters of John*, 70.

humanity. When God forgives us for violating his design, he pours his life into us; and that restores our capacity to connect, first with him, then with others. He makes us alive with the actual life of Christ. The energy with which Jesus heard and obeyed the Father, the impulses that lay behind everything he did—his tenderness with the lame man, his indignation with the moneychangers, his patience with Phillip, his red-hot scorn of the Pharisees, his love for children, his resolve to endure injustice without compliant—are in us. *The impulses that energized Jesus's life on earth are actually in us.* That's part of what it means to be alive in Christ.[5]

Once again, the italics are Crabb's, used to emphasize this astonishing reality. And this truth is absolutely essential to the message the Apostles shared everywhere they went. As John implores in his letter,

> See that what you have heard from the beginning remains in you. If it does, you also will remain in the Son and in the Father. And this is what he promised us—eternal life . . . The anointing you received from him remains in you, and you do not need anyone to teach you. But as his anointing teaches you about all things and as that anointing is real . . . just as it has taught you, remain in him. (2:24, 27)

Notice how often John uses the phrase "remain in." What John is speaking of is profoundly mysterious and spiritual. John fills his letter with the idea of our being in Christ and Christ being in us. He encourages the same intimate relationship with Jesus that Jesus himself encourages, as recorded in John 15:4–5:

> Remain in me, as I also remain in you. No branch can bear fruit by itself; it must remain in the vine. Neither can you bear fruit unless you remain in me. I am the vine; you are the branches. If you remain in me and I in you, you will bear much fruit; apart from me you can do nothing.

5. Crabb, *Connecting*, 35–6.

Paul lists some of this fruit in his letter to the Galatians: love, joy, peace, patience, kindness, goodness, faithfulness, gentleness, and self-control. We don't produce these from our own will or effort. They grow from Christ dwelling in us. We don't make it happen; we let it happen.

The key word in all of this is the Greek word *menō*, which means to "remain," "dwell," or "abide." For restless Americans, it can be difficult to live into this word because it leaves us nothing to do, at least actively—the verb is even stated in the passive voice. The more we simply abide in Christ, and let Christ abide in us, the more we begin to reflect and resemble Christ. The more we abide in Christ, and let Christ abide in us, the more we tend to "obey" his commands because of the power of the Spirit that is at work within us. Rather than expending our energy trying to rid ourselves of the weeds in our lives, like Benjamin Franklin tried, we allow the energy of the Spirit of Christ to bear fruit in our lives.

John does not claim that he has any unique inspiration on these matters. Rather, in 2:20–21, he admits, "all of you know the truth. I do not write to you because you do not know the truth, but because you do know it." John Calvin understands the intent of John's words in this letter as follows: "The Apostle . . . reminded them of things already known, and also exhorted them to rouse up the sparks of the Spirit, that a full brightness might shine forth in them."[6]

In our own time, the psychiatrist David Burns has shed light on the effect such reminders can have in our lives. In his book *Feeling Good*, Dr. Burns outlines the theory and practice of cognitive therapy.[7] In pathetically brief summation (my apologies, Dr. Burns), cognitive therapy asks us to listen to our thoughts and to believe that what we tell ourselves affects what we feel and do. According to the cognitive therapy model, if our thoughts are distorted or false, our feelings and actions will likewise be distorted and destructive. If what we tell ourselves is based in truth, our feelings

6. Calvin, *Commentaries*, 193.

7. Burns, David. *Feeling Good: The New Mood Therapy*. New York: Avon, 1980.

and actions will be constructive and helpful. John is a biblical prac-
titioner of cognitive therapy, imploring us to remind ourselves of
the truth we know so that we might share in the life of God. He
essentially breaks out in a song full of truths to abide in:

> I am writing to you, dear children,
>> because your sins have been forgiven
>>> on account of his name.
> I am writing to you, fathers,
>> because you know him who is from
>>> the beginning.
> I am writing to you, young men,
>> because you have overcome the evil
>>> one.
> I write to you, dear children,
>> because you know the Father.
> I write to you, fathers,
>> because you know him who is from the
>>> beginning.
> I write to you, young men,
>> because you are strong,
>> and the word of God lives in you,
>> and you have overcome the evil one. (2:12–14)

Though in the convention of his time John wrote using
gender-exclusive nouns and pronouns, we know that these exhor-
tations truly include all God's children—mothers, fathers, daugh-
ters, sons, female, male and all along the spectrum. God lives in us.
We know this. In the words of another song, this one by the boys
from Liverpool, let it be.

For those of us who are tired of battling our own worst selves,
John's words are like the wave of a white flag after a long, tiresome
siege. John reminds us that we are anointed with the Spirit of truth.
Christ is alive in us! John exhorts us to let it be, to let the life of
Christ take over, to abide in him and let him abide in us.

I'll close this chapter with the words of another pastor, George
Herbert, an Anglican priest from seventeenth-century England.
Though the title, "Love (III)," is rather utilitarian, the heart of the
poem beautifully glorifies the life we are called to by, and in, Christ:

Love bade me welcome: yet my soul drew back,
    Guilty of dust and sin.
But quick-ey'd Love, observing me grow slack
    From my first entrance in,
Drew nearer to me, sweetly questioning,
    If I lack'd anything.

A guest, I answer'd, worthy to be here:
    Love said, You shall be he.
I the unkind, ungrateful? Ah my dear,
    I cannot look on thee.
Love took my hand, and smiling did reply,
    Who made the eyes but I?

Truth Lord, but I have marr'd them: let my shame
    Go where it doth deserve.
And know you not, says Love, who bore the blame?
    My dear, then I will serve.
You must sit down, says Love, and taste my meat:
    So I did sit and eat.[8]

Like many of us, Herbert believes that his sinful acts will bar him from entering the kingdom of God; or, that he must do something worthy—he must "serve"—to gain entrance. Love proclaims that neither of these beliefs is true. Herbert simply needs to sit with the God of life, abide in the presence of Christ; and, let Christ abide with him. The same holds true for us all.

8. Herbert, *The Temple*, 316.

## Chapter Six

# Embracing the Family Name

*See what great love the Father has lavished on us, that we should be called children of God! And that is what we are! The reason the world does not know us is that it did not know him. Dear friends, now we are children of God, and what we will be has not yet been made known. But we know that when Christ appears, we shall be like him, for we shall see him as he is.* (1 *John* 3:1–2)

I will confess that in the eyes of some of my brothers and sisters in the Christian faith, I have danced on a slippery slope. My offense? I read *Harry Potter and the Sorcerer's Stone*. And I liked it. And then I read the rest of the series, which I liked so much, I read it aloud to my children until they were able to read it themselves. One time, I even brought one of the books into the sanctuary and read from it to the congregation—from the pulpit!

When the series was fresh on the best-seller lists, I actually read of some people in the family of God who believed that J. K. Rowling's muse was a demon. Their condemnations of the Harry Potter series no longer bellow from the church steeples, but the magic and witches and potions within Rowling's pages still seem to overwhelm some Christians with fear. I don't feel much need to participate in Potter apologetics, but I believe these frightened folks are missing out on the heart of the story—they are missing out on Rowling's affirmation of such biblical virtues as self-sacrifice, faithfulness in friendship, and choosing good over evil.

From my perch on the slippery slope, I read the Harry Potter series as a contemporary fairy tale. At the center of the story, we find the classic fairy tale conundrum of a case of mistaken identity. Whether they feature a frog who is really a prince, an ugly duckling who is really a swan, or a poor, orphan girl whose father is actually alive and very rich, many of the stories we first learn and cherish are ones that whisper to us, "You may not be who others, even you, think you are."

Frederick Buechner, an author and Presbyterian minister, first enlightened me on this characteristic of fairy tales in his book *Telling the Truth*. He writes,

> As far as I know, there has never been an age that has not produced fairy tales. . . Different as they are from each other, they seem to have certain features in common . . . There seems reason to believe that if nothing else, they have something to tell us about the kind of things we keep on dreaming century after century, in good times and bad . . . Maybe above all they are tales about transformation where all creatures are revealed in the end as what they truly are . . . They are tales of transformation where the ones who live happily ever after, as by no means everybody does in fairy tales, are transformed into what they have it in them at their best to be.[1]

Part of the reason the Harry Potter stories are so popular, I believe, is that through them we hear a voice whispering, "What is true of Harry Potter, may be true of you. You may not be who others, or even you, think you are."

For those of you who haven't yet tumbled down the Harry Potter slope, here are the basics concerning Harry's fairy tale. Within the first several pages we learn that Harry lives with his

1. Buechner, *Truth*, 75–76, 79–80.

aunt, uncle, and cousin, the Dursleys, in a suburban home in England. The only thing he has been told about his parents is that they died in a car accident. The Dursleys are a cruel lot. They treat Harry despicably, making him sleep in a storage closet under the stairs, letting him go hungry quite often. And then one evening, while the Dursleys and Harry are staying on a remote Scottish isle, a large giant bursts in on them:

> Harry looked up at the giant . . . "Who are you?"
>
> "True, I haven't introduced meself. Rubeus Hagrid, Keeper of Keys and Grounds at Hogwarts . . . yeh'll know all about Hogwarts, o'course."
>
> "Er—no," said Harry.
>
> Hagrid looked shocked.
>
> "Sorry," Harry said quickly.
>
> "*Sorry*?" barked Hagrid, turning to stare at the Dursleys, who shrank back into the shadows. "It's them as should be sorry! . . . Did yeh never wonder where yer parent's learned it all?"
>
> "All what?" asked Harry.
>
> "ALL WHAT?" Hagrid thundered. "Now wait jus' one second! . . . Do you mean ter tell me," he growled at the Dursleys, "that this boy—this boy!—knows nothin' abou'—about ANYTHING?"
>
> Harry thought this was going a bit far. He had been to school, after all, and his marks weren't bad.
>
> "I know *some* things," he said. "I can, you know, do math and stuff."
>
> But Hagrid simply waved his hand and said, "About *our* world, I mean. *Your* world. *My* world. *Yer parents'* world . . . Yeh must know about yer mom and dad," he said. "I mean, they're *famous*. You're *famous*."
>
> "What? My—my mom and dad weren't famous, were they?"
>
> "Yeh don' know . . . yeh don' know . . ." Hagrid ran his fingers though his hair, fixing Harry with a bewildered stare.
>
> "Yeh don' know what yeh *are*?" he said finally . . . "Harry—yer a wizard."
>
> "I'm a *what*?" gasped Harry.

> "A wizard, o' course," said Hagrid, sitting back down on the sofa, which groaned and sank even lower, "an' a thumpin' good'un, I'd say, once yeh've been trained up a bit. With a mum an' dad like yours, what else would yeh be?"[2]

Throughout this story, and the stories that follow, Harry gradually discovers more and more about his true identity and that of his parents. By the end of the series, Harry has fully embraced his family's heritage, his own skills as a wizard, and all that his new identity entails.

While not promising the same extraordinary powers Harry possesses as part of his true identity, one of the key purposes of John's letter, which we have been considering, is to reveal to his readers their own true identities. In 3:2, John straightforwardly proclaims, "Dear friends, now we are children of God." John Stott in his commentary on this passage asserts that this identification, "children of God," "is no mere title; it is a fact."[3]

In 3:1, the NIV leaves out a translation of the Greek word *idete*. Leaving it out, however, misses the tenor of John's exclamation. And that missing word packs power; when translated into English, it exhorts us to "Behold!" John is emphatically asking us to stop whatever else we are doing and to think about this astonishing revelation: "How great is the love the Father has lavished on us, that we should be called children of God! And that is what we are!" The Prologue to John's Gospel goes so far as to assert that a significant reason Jesus, the anointed one, came to dwell with us was to establish this identity for all who are willing to embrace it. Many of us focus all too narrowly on the forgiveness of sins that Christ brought. This is a key message, yet Christ came for far more than that. Christ came to reunite us with our true family:

> He was in the world, and though the world was made through him, the world did not recognize him. He came to that which was his own, but his own did not receive him. Yet to all who did receive him, to those who

2. Rowling, *Harry Potter*, 48–51.
3. Stott, *Letters of John*, 122.

believed in his name, he gave the right to become children of God—children born not of natural descent, nor
of human decision or a husband's will, but born of God.
(1:10–13)

Perhaps we've been living with the Dursleys too long, but
this proclamation can be hard to trust, to believe and embrace.
John's Prologue earlier acknowledges that "The light shines in the
darkness, and the darkness has not overcome it" (1:5). Literally,
the darkness has not "grasped" it. Or, again, as quoted above, "He
came to that which was his own, but his own did not receive him."
It is no surprise, then, that others frequently miss our family re-
semblance with God through Christ. In his letter, John notes, "The
reason the world does not know us is it did not know him" (3:1). If
the world didn't recognize the family characteristics in Jesus, why
should we expect they, or even we, would see them in us?

Again, I come back to the importance and power of that
little word *idete*, or "behold." Look hard. Focus. As John Calvin
professes:

> It is a trial that grievously assaults our faith, that we are
> not so much regarded as God's children, or that no mark
> of so great an excellency appears in us, but that, on the
> contrary . . . as to our body we are dust and a shadow,
> and death is always before our eyes; we are also subject
> to a thousand miseries and the soul is exposed to innu-
> merable evils . . . The more necessary it is that all our
> thoughts should be withdrawn from the present view of
> things, lest the miseries . . . should shake our faith in that
> felicity which as yet lies hid.[4]

Oh that we might know this truth within our souls—the truth
of who we really are. Calvin encourages the same awareness of our
identity as does John. So, in case our reading glasses were a little
smudged or we were block reading the first time, I will quote John
again, "See what great love the Father has lavished on us, that we
should be called children of God! And that is what we are!" (3:1)
We are God's children.

4. Calvin, *Commentaries*, 203–4.

The more we become aware of our identity as God's children, the more we can then look for the ways in which we reveal our inherited "family" traits. As God's children we can expect to reflect, at least in glimpses, characteristics of our divine parents, God our Mother and Father. Even in our earthly families, it can be surprising how much we resemble our parents, without even trying. Early on in his memoir *All Over But the Shoutin'*, Rick Bragg notes this connection with his mother:

> I am proud of who and what I am, just as proud of being the son of a woman who picked cotton and took in ironing as I am of working in a place like the *New York Times*. I have always believed that one could not have been without the other . . . I hope [my momma] sees some of her backbone in me, . . . She was the one who taught me not to give a damn when it hurt. I hope she sees some of her gentleness and sensitivity in my words, because if there is any of that in me still, it came from her. In an important way, her sadness is in every story I write."[5]

But what brought Bragg's story to mind was the way in which, much later in the story, he also reveals the characteristics of his father in himself, regrettable as that may be. The following is written by Bragg, as if to his father directly:

> I hear it said a lot . . . what a good man I turned out to be, considering . . . The truth is that, in so many ways, I am just like you. The meanness you had in you, I used to get where I am. But instead of spraying it out, like you did, I channeled it . . . I used your coldness, the same way I used my momma's kindness, in my work . . . Your hatred of responsibility, of ties, is in me just as strong as it was in you.[6]

Fortunately for us, the family traits we have inherited from God are those that are revealed most distinctly in Jesus—love, joy, peace, patience, kindness, goodness, faithfulness, gentleness, and

5. Bragg, *Shoutin'*, xx.
6. Ibid, 318.

self-control. When we see these characteristics displayed in our lives, we are reminded of our true identity.

And there's more. For all that this identity means for us here and now—for the ways in which we see faint glimmers of Christ in our words and deeds here and now—ultimately it will mean a complete transformation. John boldly promises, "What we will be has not yet been made known. But we know that when [Christ] appears, we shall be like him, for we shall see him as he is" (3:2). Through the life, death, and resurrection of Jesus, with the work of the Spirit, we are brought into a familial relationship with God the Father, God the Mother. Jesus, therefore, becomes, as Calvin puts it, "a perfect pattern of our purity."[7] One day, we will fully reflect the traits of our true family.

My temptation, at this point, is to end this chapter by proposing that we all follow in our family's footsteps, that we look to the great works of Jesus and emulate them in our own lives. But rather than focusing on what we ought to do, I believe that God first wants us to embrace who we are. Over and over again throughout the Scriptures, God begins with a revelation of our status, before ever talking about our service. Even the Ten Commandments are preceded by a revelation of where we stand in relationship to God: "I am the Lord your God, who brought you out of Egypt, out of the land of slavery" (Exod 20:2). Before laying down the law, God reminds us of our close relationship, of the deep love shown to us by the gracious act of bringing us out of a land of slavery. All subsequent acts flow from that prior relationship. Our priority, then, is to know who we are and embrace our identity.

Years ago, I was asked to officiate the memorial service for a dearly loved mother of three adult children. She died after eighty years of a life well-lived. While gathered with the family to share stories and talk about the service, one of the sons urged his sister, "Tell him what she used to say to us whenever we were about to leave the house on a date."

The sister and other brother immediately recognized the experience to which he was referring. As they were getting ready to

7. Calvin, *Commentaries*, 207.

leave on a date, or to a party, their mother would stand patiently by the front door. She never gave them a curfew. She never told them to beware of booze, drugs, or the ways of the flesh. But as they opened the door to leave, she would simply give them a great big hug, look them in the eyes, and say, "Remember who you are." That's it.

As we go about our lives, God embraces us with love and graciously says to us, "Remember who you are."

## Chapter Seven

# Love Is a Verb

*This is how we know what love is: Jesus Christ laid down his life for us. And we ought to lay down our lives for our brothers and sisters. If anyone has material possessions and sees a brother or sister in need but has no pity on them, how can the love of God be in that person? Dear children, let us not love with words or speech but with actions and in truth. (1 John 3:16–18)*

Through my roughly two decades as a pastor, I've gone back and forth on whether I think there is value to creating church mission statements. For a while, experts in the corporate world considered mission statements absolutely essential to the successful operation of an organization and an efficient use of its resources. Yet it's tough to craft a mission statement that passes the smell test, a mission statement that manages to juggle both substance and distinctiveness. And if we're speaking specifically about creating a mission statement for a congregation, we've got the obvious problem that most of the good ones are already taken: God has already provided some pretty significant options in the Scriptures.

For instance, in 3:11, John spins out a fairly promising candidate for a congregational mission statement with the following, "This is the message you heard from the beginning: We should love one another." This mission statement has the added advantage of being one that John's boss has already approved. "This is my command," says Jesus, himself, "Love each other." So John took a little liberty with the "one another" versus the "each other." Close enough.

At first, though, this mission statement might seem vapid. Doesn't it sound fairly weak? "Love one another." I see a circle of multiethnic people of all ages, their faces smiling and their hands linked together as they stand in a field of wild flowers, a soft ballad from Air Supply playing in the background. Without additional context, these words from John have almost no substance. But John does, in fact, go on to provide us with further explanation, and in reading what he writes, I'm not so sure I want to know what he means. The way he explains it, I find that I'm the one who is weak, not the substance of love or its value as a mission statement.

John follows his reminder of our mission with an immediate warning about love's opposite: "Do not be like Cain, who belonged to the evil one and murdered his brother" (3:12). In the story of Cain and Abel both brothers bring offerings to God. God approves of Abel's offering, but not Cain's. In a jealous rage, Cain kills his brother. God shows up after the murder, looking for Abel and asks Cain if he knows where to find Abel. Cain, in turn, questions God, "Am I my brother's keeper?" (Gen 4:9) The way John fleshes out the meaning of "love" in this passage, we learn that the answer is "Yes!"

Rather than at least simply letting his brother alone, Cain took the way all too often emulated by the world. In commenting on John's reference to Cain, D. Moody Smith makes the case that the way of Cain is certainly often emulated by too many in the United States:

> In America we live in a society plagued by murder, one in which the leading cause of death among young men of certain ages and ethnic groups is murder. Thousands upon thousands of Americans are murdered each year, from children in cribs to the elderly in their homes.[1]

1. Smith, *John*, 92.

John notes that far more of us may be implicated in the way of Cain than those who physically shoot, stab, or otherwise kill someone, writing that even "Anyone who hates a brother or sister is a murderer" (3:15). Most of us take the word *hate* somewhat lightly; we use it casually, to say things like "I hate the 49ers" or "I hate mealy apples." Still, every now and again, we hear the violence lurking in the word. When a child says she hates Brussel sprouts, no big thing, but we cringe when a child spits at another child, shouting "I hate you!" We are then shocked by the venom the word holds. The way of the world, the way of Cain, the way of war, hatred, and murder—it all leads to death.

Ironically, when John moves us away from what love is not and toward what love is, death still looms as a possibility, but its meaning changes entirely: "This is how we know what love is: Jesus Christ laid down his life for us" (3:16). By sacrificing his life, Jesus defines love for us. He is the standard by which every other definition of love must be judged. In the tragic and beautiful novel, *The Grapes of Wrath*, John Steinbeck alludes to Jesus Christ as he fashions his own understanding of the fullness of love. Steinbeck writes of a disillusioned preacher named Jim Casey who lays down his life for the sake of others. Midway through the story, we read of Casey defending the lives of several destitute migrant men by clubbing a corrupt policeman, knocking him unconscious. Casey shoos the men away saying, "Go on, get out . . . Somebody got to take the blame. I got no kids. They'll jus' put me in jail, an' I ain't doin' nothin' but set aroun."[2] Later in the story, after again defending the oppressed, Casey is beaten to death with an axe handle. It is no coincidence then that Casey, who offers himself in supreme acts of love, shares the same initials (in terms of our popular understanding) as Jesus Christ. Throughout the centuries, countless artists and philosophers have considered Jesus the greatest illustration of love ever, regardless of their belief or doubt of his divinity.

When John proclaims, "This is how we know what love is: Jesus Christ laid down his life for us," he frighteningly goes on to say, "And we ought to lay down our lives for our brothers and

2. Steinbeck, *Grapes of Wrath*, 276.

sisters" (3:16). We all too often, and all too quickly, dismiss this exhortation as hyperbole on John's part. Yet the majority of the Apostles died professing their faith, and thousands of early followers of Christ died professing their faith. I believe we ought to attend to these words with great care.

Years ago, I read an article in *Time* magazine about a man named William Wylie Tomes Jr., a man who took these words to heart in profound ways. After being raised in upper-class Evanston, Illinois and working through a master's degree, Tomes had two very good job offers in the Chicago area. While praying in St. Joseph's Ukrainian Catholic Church about which offer to accept, Tomes had a very powerful experience. Tomes had not had a particularly deep or abiding faith, yet on that day, Tomes recounts, "When I knelt down, everything turned fuzzy except the face of Christ on a painting near the altar." Tomes then heard the words of Christ: "Love. You are forbidden to do anything other than that."[3]

The journey that began with those words later led him to give up everything he owned, literally, and begin working with gangs in the infamous Cabrini-Green housing project. When the article was published, Tomes, nicknamed Brother Bill by the gang members, had walked into the midst of gunfire over fifty times; he had risked his life in order to make it stop, in order to bring peace. And he had been successful each time. The article quoted a twenty-six-year-old gang member named Antonio who said, "It's like if Brother Bill is willing to take a bullet because he loves you that much, it makes it harder for you to hate the other side. I think that's why the shooting stops."[4] The writer of the article, Ron Stodgill, makes the following observation:

> His vulnerability, his willingness to put his life on the line, his unconditional offering of acceptance and forgiveness and, yes, love are a constant source of astonishment for men and boys weaned on hate and rejection. "I think he's

3. Stodgill, "Line of Fire," *TIME*, August 24, 2002.
4. Ibid.

an angel," says a twenty-two-year-old Vice Lord. "I really think God sent him here."[5]

Few of us will ever have the calling—or the courage—that William Tomes has. Still, John challenges us with another way of loving that most of us are in a position to fulfill, at least potentially, almost every day. John writes in 3:17: "If anyone has material possessions and sees a brother or sister in need but has no pity on them, how can the love of God be in that person?" In some ways, this question becomes an even greater challenge than the challenge to lay down our lives, because we face this situation all the time. In fact, John Stott points out that the challenge becomes even more specific to our daily lives as John narrows his focus from laying down our lives for our "brothers and sisters"—plural—to seeing one, singular "brother" or "sister" in need.[6] John's understanding of love is not weak at all; it is strong and costly.

While living in Vancouver, British Columbia, as a grad student I once witnessed a beautiful illustration of someone answering this challenge. One of my classmates and I were walking on a vibrant, posh stretch of Granville Street when a person sitting on the sidewalk stretched out a grubby hand and asked if we had any spare change. I had gone to the University of Washington in Seattle for my undergraduate degree and had plenty of experience being accosted by panhandlers while walking the Ave, so I ignored the grubby hand and the request and continued walking. My classmate, Mike, stopped and responded, "Hey, I make it a practice not to hand out cash, but if you've got the time, I'd be more than happy to take you to get something to eat or buy you some groceries at the store." I was shocked. I knew that Mike didn't have much money himself, and although we weren't in a big hurry to get anywhere, this could have taken a while. The man took him up on the offer. We all walked over to a 7–11 nearby, and Mike paid for a bag of grocery items that the man had picked out himself. I'd never seen this done before, and I'd never even thought of doing anything

5. Ibid.
6. Stott, *Letters of John*, 145.

along the same lines. Mike saw "a brother in need" and gave some of his own "material possessions" to help him out.

This is the content of love as John understands it. At the same time, we need to remember which end of the truck we attach the trailer to. On our own, we have neither the wisdom nor the strength to sustain acts of love. As I explored in the previous chapter, if our focus is on the action itself, we will quickly tire. As Jesus reminds us in his vital parable of the Vine and the Branches, "Remain in me, as I also remain in you. No branch can bear fruit by itself; it must remain in the vine. Neither can you bear fruit unless you remain in me" (John 15:4). When we attend to Christ dwelling within us, when we let his love fill us, we will love in response. When we abide in Christ, and Christ abides in us, as I once heard Dallas Willard phrase it in a lecture, "God's commands turn out to be promises, promises that 'We can be like this.'" When we are hitched to God's love and presence, then we can find joy in John's command: "Dear children, let us not love with words or tongue but with actions and in truth" (3:18).

With all of this in mind, I return to the mission statement of 3:11, "Love one another," and I am beginning to understand the tremendous richness of this call to action. Rather than being vapid and weak, this mission calls us to a powerful co-mission with Jesus Christ to restore and reconcile. As Brother Bill humbly professed, "I am an ordinary man with an extraordinary mission."[7] In one of the collected sermons of the Rev. Peter J. Gomes, he captured the essence of what is at stake in our living out of this mission:

> I do not believe that God moves in thunderstorms or speaks in the accents of natural disasters. I do not believe that God interferes in the often tragic course of the world's activity; I do not believe that God is a great puppeteer who somehow pulls the strings for good or for bad, depending upon his temper or ours. Rather, I believe that God has made the world and loves it so much that he has given himself into our hands and thus made his work our opportunity. God has chosen not to act in

7. Stodgill, "Line of Fire," *TIME*, August 24, 2002.

the form of phenomena; he has chosen now to act in the form of men and women who know him, love him, and serve him. By God's love for us in Jesus Christ we are become in ourselves, in our own persons, in our daily work acts of God, evidence, living proof that the God who acted in the lives of the prophets, the martyrs, and the saints still acts in the likes and the lives of us.[8]

We are called into a mission that will change the world: "Love one another."

8. Gomes, *Sermons*, 179.

## Chapter Eight

# Christian Spirituality

*This is how we know that he lives in us: We know it by the*
*Spirit he gave us. (1 John 3:24)*

The declaration "I'm not religious, but I am spiritual" has
become quite popular of late. People who feel this way and
who live in Seattle, as I do, ought to consider themselves quite
fortunate. Seattle offers a veritable cornucopia of spirituality. In
fact, at one point not too long ago, on one relatively short stretch
of street in the northeast part of the city, a person could find, as
reported by the *Seattle Times*, "Tibetan Buddhism, Siberian sha-
manism, a Church of Self-Realization. Meditation, yoga, chanting.
Psychics, palm readers, astrologists. Reiki, Rolfing, reflexology.
Acupuncture, colonics, detoxification. Naturopathy, homeopathy,
aromatherapy. Christianity, Judaism, Hinduism."[1] Something for
everyone.

I was glad to see Christianity included in the enumeration of
spirituality on that street. We may think of Christianity as primarily a religion, but to be truly Christian means to be deeply spiritual.
Returning to a passage I cited earlier in this book, Jesus, himself,
acknowledged this essential aspect of discipleship:

1. Janet I. Tu, "65th and Divine," *Seattle Times*, April 2, 2000.

> If you love me, keep my commands. And I will ask the
> Father, and he will give you another advocate to help
> you and be with you forever—the Spirit of truth. The
> world cannot accept him, because it neither sees him nor
> knows him. But you know him, for he lives with you and
> will be in you . . . On that day you will realize that I am
> in my Father, and you are in me, and I am in you. (John
> 14:15–17, 20)

That is some hard-core, haunted house "wooOOooowOOOoo"
spiritual stuff. John echoes this essential spirituality in his letter:
"Those who obey [Christ's] commands live in him, and he in them.
And this is how we know that he lives in us: We know by the Spirit
he gave us" (3:24).

Interestingly, both Jesus and John tie spirituality, which could
be rather abstract, together with obeying Christ's commands, a
concrete act. Yet for both of them, this obedience does not draw
the Spirit into us; rather, our obedience flows out of our spiritual
communion with God. In essence, obedience results from Christ
abiding in us and our abiding in Christ. We prepare a meal for
homeless families because our heart stirs us to action by the presence of Christ's spirit; our act of service does not inspire Jesus to
take up an abode within our hearts. John Stott adds to our understanding of how this works: "Abiding in Christ' is not a mystical
experience which anyone may claim; its indispensable accompani-
ments are the confession of Jesus as the son of God come in the
flesh, and a consistent life of holiness and love . . . The Spirit . . .
manifests himself objectively in our life and conduct."[2] As we have
seen so often in John's understanding of discipleship, attending to
God's abiding presence within us is the wellspring from which
good works flow.

As alluded to above, the more we attend to the movements
of God's spirit within us, the more we will exhibit ourselves as
Christs disciples. And though it expresses itself outwardly, this attentive discipleship is foremost a profoundly interior experience.
Earl Palmer points out, "We know the abiding presence of Jesus

---

2. Stott, *Letters of John*, 152.

Christ in our lives because of the inward confirmation of the Holy Spirit."[3] Stott adds, "The indwelling Holy Spirit's anointing . . . impart[s] a built-in spiritual instinct."[4]

By nature, as human beings, we are a mysterious hybrid of spirit and flesh. In order to live full, whole, healthy lives, we require nourishment of both body and soul. For most of us, understanding that the body needs nourishment comes quite naturally. Yet we may not be as aware that the same is true for our souls. Perhaps the best illustration for how this nourishment of our spiritual lives might work comes from researchers at my alma mater, the University of Washington. Some very bright minds there have figured out a way to use ambient backscatter—the myriad electrical signals that bombard the atmosphere we live in—to power tiny communications devices as part of a sensory network. As blogger Dave Reinhardt explains:

> The ambient backscatter devices are not equipped with an independent power source. They are not outfitted with batteries of any kind . . . they are designed in such a way that, when they are in the presence of the right signals, they 'come alive.' The power they receive from these signals causes them to literally light up and . . . enables them to communicate with other similar devices.[5]

Reinhardt then poses a series of rhetorical questions that lead in the direction toward connecting the way these devices work with the way our spiritual lives work:

> What if, at the most basic, creaturely level, each person is utterly dependent on the animating, sustaining power of God not merely to live, but to live fully? What if we are more like these circuit boards than we care to imagine: lifeless and mute until we receive and then reflect the ever-present, ambient (and glorious) signal of God in Christ?[6]

3. Palmer, *1, 2, 3 John*, 59.
4. Stott, *Letters of John*, 152.
5. Reinhardt, "Power and Glory," Transpositions.
6. Ibid.

I believe that we can skip the hypothetical scenario and simply concede that without the breath of God within us, we may have a physical existence, but we are not fully alive. Therefore, those who claim a "spiritual" self, religiously or not, sense a vital truth.

So, we live now in a time rich with a bountiful variety of nourishment for the body and spiritual practices for the soul, a time reawakened to the importance of our spiritual selves as well as our physical selves. And that is cause to rejoice. All followers of Christ can gladly join in with those who proudly proclaim, "I am spiritual." To be truly Christian is to be deeply spiritual; it is to be attentive and attuned to the Spirit dwelling within us. It means listening for the Spirit in our hearts and minds and allowing the Spirit to empower us and guide us in our work in the world.

At the same time, John warns us that being spiritual requires some discernment in order to be healthy. In 4:1, John adds, "Dear friends, do not believe every spirit, but test the spirits to see whether they are from God." John lived in a time and place where spirituality was also very popular. Unfortunately, some people used the popularity of spirituality to lead followers down unhealthy and destructive paths. John refers to these leaders as "false prophets." There are many leaders today who, similarly, offer us direction on our path to connecting with Jesus and communing with God. Some are earnest, but some are in it for themselves. Some may lead us to a deeper communion with Jesus, but some may send us on paths fraught with destruction.

One group of false prophets who were influencing people during the time of his writing particularly angered John—the gnostics. They claimed to have a unique connection to the spiritual realm and to have secret knowledge about God. As one expression of this, they claimed to "know" that Jesus did not receive the Holy Spirit until his baptism as an adult and that the Spirit left him at his death. In other words, they believed that Jesus and the Christ were not one and the same, and they claimed to have received this revelation from the Spirit of God. John would have none of it. He adds in his letter, "This is how you can recognize the Spirit of God: Every spirit that acknowledges that Jesus Christ has come in the flesh is from God, but every spirit that does not acknowledge Jesus is not from God" (4:2–3). Jesus, his office as the Christ, and the Holy Spirit cannot be separated.

In a passage from John's Gospel that I cited earlier, when Jesus promises the Spirit of truth he adds the following:

> All this I have spoken while still with you. But the Advocate, the Holy Spirit, whom the Father will send in my name, will teach you all things and will remind you of everything I have said to you. (14:25–26)

Notice the essential connection between the Spirit, Jesus—his "name" and words—and the Spirit's work. Spirituality in the Christian faith is not a matter of simply clearing out the chaotic thoughts of the mind and finding some kind of inner peace, or connecting to any given presence in the spiritual realm; it is a spirituality that finds its center in Jesus, specifically—in his life, his words, and his continued presence through the Holy Spirit. Spirituality in the Christian tradition has always believed that the spirit and body of Jesus were unified; and, therefore, our spirituality as followers of Christ should seek that same unity of spirit and body in Christ. For example, one of the classic works on spirituality in the Christian church, *The Spiritual Exercises of St. Ignatius*, teaches readers to meditate on scenes from the life of Jesus as recorded in the Gospels.[7] Ignatius encourages us to imagine the scenes with our senses: What sounds do we hear? What do we feel with our touch? What do we smell? What do we taste? Such exercises as these unite body and soul in a distinctly Christian spiritual experience.

Truly Christian spirituality always leads us closer to Jesus, the Christ of the scriptures; the Jesus of love and grace, the Son of God and the Son of Man. In fact, truly Christian spirituality unites us, body and soul, with Jesus Christ in such a way that we will find

---

7. Ignatius, *The Spiritual Exercises of Saint Ignatius*, translated by Pierre Wolff, Ligouri, MO: Ligouri / Triumph, 1997.

ourselves outwardly expressing the love of Christ that we experience within. It will lead us closer to our neighbor, to our brothers and sisters, to those in need. If we find ourselves increasingly self-focused and self-centered, it is likely that we are not spending time with the Spirit of Christ. When we find ourselves increasing in love for and understanding of Christ and our neighbor—what John may call obedience—then we know that we are spending time with the Spirit of Christ. That is Christian spirituality.

# Chapter Nine

# Love Is a Noun

*And so we know and rely on the love God has for us. God is love. Whoever lives in love lives in God, and God in them. (1 John 4:16)*

I was almost a monk. Well, never through any formal religious order. And I didn't bother considering the vow of poverty, or silence. But I was ready for the vow of chastity.

I had a four-year run in the late eighties where I felt like I was living the lyrics of the old Mickey Gilley song where he sings of, "Lookin' for love in all the wrong places." I'd fall for some new person, try to avoid my feelings because of previous bad experiences, finally give in, make some sort of overture, and—SLAM! Rejection. And the try-a-few-dates-and-it-doesn't-work-out rejections apparently weren't good enough for me; I inevitably received the Oh-that's-sweet-but-I've-decided-to-go-back-to-my-old-boyfriend-and-marry-him type of rejections. After thinking about my relationship failures for a long time, I announced to my closest friends, in utmost seriousness, "I think God is trying to tell me I'm supposed to be single and celibate the rest of my life." They laughed.

They laughed because they knew me well enough to see my announcement as sincere, yet short-sighted. I think they also laughed because they are human beings and knew how important intimate love is for almost all human beings. I believe God rarely—rarely!—calls anyone to be single and celibate. The vast majority of us are not at our best on our own; and the vast majority of us deeply desire an intimate relationship of love. Just turn on the radio. Look at the books that people *actually* read—romance novels are best sellers! Think of the movies and TV shows we watch. And, if you add in sex as a derivative of love, it's pretty clear that love, in its variety of forms, is one of the greatest fixations of our species. Yet for all the attention we give love, we have tremendous difficulty finding it, especially in its life-altering form.

In John's understanding, love originates from God. He writes, "Dear friends, let us love one another, for love comes from God. Everyone who loves has been born of God and knows God. Whoever does not love does not know God, because God is love" (4:7–8). In relation to John's profession above, the Scottish theologian James Torrance once gave a series of lectures in Manchester on the topic of the Trinity. In one of the lectures, Torrance tied the origination of love in God to God's being three persons in one—Father, Son and Holy Spirit. He contended:

> At the center of the New Testament stands . . . a unique relationship [between the three persons of the Trinity] . . . This unique relationship is described as one of mutual love, mutual self-giving, mutual testifying, mutual glorifying . . . of mutual 'indwelling' (*perichōrēsis*, to use the word of the ancient church).[1]

In a later lecture, Torrance continues:

> Love always implies a communion between persons, and we have seen that in our Christian doctrine of God. The Father loves the Son in the communion of the Spirit. The Son loves the Father in the communion of the Spirit. God has his being-in-communion. This triune God has in grace created us as male and female in his image, that

1. Torrance, *Triune God*, 30–32.

we might find our true being in intimate communion with him and with one another. He created us for *communio* to be 'co-lovers' (*condiligentes*).[2]

So love is in the very being of God and we were originally created as an expression of that love.

Of course, this all happened before our time, in pre-history so to speak. Thus, John reminds us of what God did, in our time, to help us understand love:

> This is how God showed his love among us: He sent his one and only Son into the world that we might live through him. This is love: not that we loved God, but that God loved us and sent his Son as an atoning sacrifice for our sins. (4:9–10)

I used to read this passage from within my own perspective as a father and the cost of giving up a child. I could not imagine loving someone so deeply that I would be willing to even consider giving up my children to save someone else's life. Reading from that perspective actually makes God sound vile, heartless. But I think reading this passage from God's side of things, the giving side, is inherently backward. *We* are the ones for whom God gave his child. God loves *us* so deeply that God was willing to give his heart away. Rather than revealing a callous God, these words reveal the depth and breadth and height of God's love for us, the immensity of God's love for *us*.

The passage we *are* supposed to read from the giver's perspective is the next line that John writes, 4:11: "Dear friends, since God so loved us, we also ought to love one another." Again, as in 4:7, John exhorts us to love one another. But between that "Dear friends" and this one, John has reminded us both of the source of love, God, and the supreme example of love, God's self-giving in Jesus. Knowing both the source and breadth of love encourages our own acts of love. And if that was not enough, John adds an astonishing promise: "No one has ever seen God; but if we love one another, God lives in us and his love is made complete in us"

2. Ibid, 72.

(4:12). In case we missed the import of these words, John Stott points out:

> It would be hard to exaggerate the greatness of this con-
> ception. It is so daring that many commentators have
> been reluctant to accept it . . . But . . . we must not stagger
> at the majesty of this conclusion. God's love, which origi-
> nates in himself and was manifested in his Son, is made
> complete in his people.[3]

We "complete" God's love. Wow! Every time I read that line from John, and Stott's affirmation of it, I am "staggered at the majesty" of it all.

I am staggered, and also emboldened. There are countless ways in which the world is desperate for God's love to be shared through us. I once heard Philip Yancey share a story about Henri Nouwen's understanding of this contemporary need of the world for us to share God's love. Nouwen was asked about his visits with AIDS patients in San Francisco. In response he said, "I saw people who were literally dying because they wanted to be loved."

For centuries, poets from all over the world have given voice to our profound desire for, and experience of, love. Some of my favorite poems on love come from poets writing in India between the fourth and tenth century. Gathered in a collection titled *Poems from the Sanskrit*, here is one example from the poet Bhartrhari:

> You are pale, friend moon, and do not sleep at night,
>     And day by day you waste away.
>     Can it be that you also
> Think only of her, as I do?[4]

Yet, one of the most beautiful love poems ever written can be found in the Hebrew Scriptures, otherwise known to Christians as the Old Testament. The Song of Songs begins:

> Let him kiss me with the kisses of his
>     mouth—
> for your love is more delightful than

3. Stott, *Letters of John*, 165.
4. Brough, *Poems*, 58.

wine.
Pleasing is the fragrance of your perfumes:
   your name is like perfume poured out.
No wonder the young women love you!
Take me away with you—let us hurry!
   Let the king bring me into his chambers. (1:1–4)

These days far too many Christians—far too many preachers, too, I believe—find this poem disturbing for its sensuality and eroticism, but throughout the history of the church, many have found a connection between the love revealed in this song and God's love for us.

Perhaps the most eloquent proponent of such a view was Bernard of Clairvaux, a twelfth-century French monk—one of those guys who really did take a vow of poverty and chastity. Bernard spent eighteen years studying, writing about, and preaching on this love poem. At one point, he wrote the following:

> It is the passionate wedding song of the soul. It is "The Song of Songs" in the same way that Jesus is "King of Kings and Lord of Lords." Only the Holy Spirit can inspire a song like this, and personal experience is the only interpreter. If you understand this mystery, enjoy! If you are not familiar with such an experience, seek to discover it rather than simply learn about it. It is not a popular song. It is inner music. It is not voices in harmony, but wills. It is not heard in streets or large crowds. It is a song for two—the bride and the groom, the lover and the loved.[5]

To know true love, Bernard would proclaim, we must know God.

I never ended up following through on becoming a monk. But as I wrote above, by March 1990, I'd had enough of romantic relationships. After four years of looking for love in all the wrong places, I offered myself to God. I said, essentially, "God, my life is yours to worry about. I'm truly giving it all up to you." Then, I signed a contract to teach English at a YMCA in Taiwan. I planned

---

5. Bernard, *Song of Songs*, 2.

to teach English to earn my keep, study Mandarin on the side, go back to mainland China where I had previously taught English, and spend the rest of my life serving God there.

A week later, a friend called me and said, "I know someone who wants to go out with you. I think you know her." He later revealed to me and that "someone" that he knew he had to be completely blunt with me or I wouldn't get the hint. On April 17, 1990, that someone and I went on our first date. Within two weeks, I had a deep inclination that she was the one I wanted to spend the rest of my life with. A little over a year later we got married, and I am happy to report that we are still together, over twenty-five years later.

I do not believe that God had been trying to tell me that he wanted me to be a monk. Rather, I believe that God was trying to tell me, "Doug, you're never going to find the love you're looking for, the fullness of love of any sort, until you turn to me, until you find the heart of love in me." Once I found love in God, I found the love of my life.

# Chapter Ten

# Real Life

*And this is the testimony: God has given us eternal life, and this life is in his Son . . . I write these things to you who believe in the name of the Son of God so that you may know that you have eternal life. (1 John 5:11, 13)*

In her mostly fascinating yet sometimes frightening book *Alone Together*, Massachusetts Institute of Technology sociologist Shirley Turkle looks at the impact technology seems to be having on both our social interactions and our understanding of life.[1] In her book, Turkle discusses Furbies and other emotionally responsive robots, reporting on the mindboggling conversations she has had with children and adults about what is "real" and what is "alive."

To most of us, the categories of "real" and "alive" might seem like obvious binaries. But Turkle illustrates that when we try to put into words what they actually are, things get murky. We know "alive" when we see it: a squirrel running is alive; a run-over squirrel is not. Yet trying to articulate clearly and succinctly these two states proves difficult.

1. Sherry Turkle, *Alone Together: Why We Expect More from Technology and Less from Each Other*, New York: Basic, 2011.

# Real Life

Search "life" digitally, or look it up in an old-school dictionary, and you will find that most definitions tend toward two categories: a biological understanding or a motivational force. Scientists focus on the first of these two definitions, the definition that *Webster's* provides as the first of many:

> 1. that property of plants and animals which makes it possible for them to take in food, get energy from it, grow, adapt themselves to their surroundings, and re-produce their kind: it is the quality that distinguishes a living animal or plant from inorganic matter or a dead organism.[2]

That's fine, as far as it goes. Still, it's probably not what we're after when we try to inspire someone with the exhortation, "You only have one life! So live *that property of plants and animals which makes it possible for you to take in food* to the fullest!" We know that there is a difference between the life of, say, a man named Doug, a Douglas fir, and a dog—or at least I hope there is. But what makes the difference?

Scientifically, not that much. The brilliant author, scientist, and professor John Medina reveals this conundrum in a story he tells in his book *The Outer Limits of Life*. He recounts a time he participated in a research group that was working to clone a gene from a blood vessel. The blood vessel was taken from a person who died in an emergency room from a massive head injury. The dead man had registered as an organ donor, so a resident was sent in to harvest a section of the aorta. I'll now let Medina tell the story himself:

> The resident beheld an eerie sight. There was a man, perfectly healthy in every way except for critical brain functions—a body fully alive and, at the same time, a person fully dead. The patient was not called a human being but was termed a heartbeating cadaver.[3]

---

2. *Webster's New World Dictionary of the American Language*, 2nd College ed., s.v., "Life."

3. Medina, *Outer Limits*, 247.

The resident brought the aorta section to the laboratory. Cells were removed and placed in petri dishes. They were then fed nutrients and antibacterial reagents and put in an incubator. Medina continues:

> The next day as we examined those living cells under the microscope, I felt those same eerie feelings. The cells were fully alive and reproducing in my petri dish, but the host and the blood vessel had long since expired. I remember wondering how science could define life when an organism was no longer living, yet possessed parts that could still be called alive. At that moment, the only difference between the human in the grave and the cells in the petri dish was their functional organization. In attempting to understand exactly what was still alive, I was forced to ask exactly what had died.[4]

So much for the biological approach.

Yet turning toward the other major grouping of definitions for *life* doesn't settle things much. These definitions seem to reach more toward what gives life rather than defining *life* itself. Again, see *Webster's*: "13. the source of vigor or liveliness [the *life* of the party] 14. vigor; liveliness; animation; vivacity."[5] If we consider magazine titles with the word *life* or *living* in them as representative of what people consider the "source" of life for themselves, we still have a long way to go to understand this phenomenon. A list of magazine titles from a brief internet search includes *Outdoor Life*, *Martha Stewart Living*, *Country Life*, *Photo Life*, *Southern Living* and even *Veggie Life*. On the positive side, this type of definition recognizes that we all have passions and interests that animate us. Yet these titles also demonstrate how this definition alone narrows our understanding of life: seeking the fullness of life in any one of our passions or interests will enhance our lives somewhat, but will leave us far from being fully alive.

4. Ibid.

5. *Webster's New World Dictionary of the American Language*, 2nd College ed., s.v., "Life."

At the end of John's letter, he warns against such misguided pursuits. As he puts it, "Dear children, keep yourselves from idols" (5:21). John uses the Greek word *eidōlon*, which in classical Greek meant "shadow" or "phantom." With these things in mind, I like Eugene Peterson's translation of this same verse in *The Message*: "Dear children, be on guard against all clever facsimiles."[6] The world offers us many clever facsimiles of life. Ultimately, however, these facsimiles—these idols—have no substance. They are shadows of the real thing. In the book of Ecclesiastes, the writer professes to have pursued every source of life the world "under the sun" has to offer; he concludes that they all amount to vapor, mist, phantoms.

As always, John returns our focus to Jesus. If we want to know life, to know the source of life, if we want to experience life and not just shadows of life, we must know and experience Christ. Chapter 5:11–12, says this most explicitly: "And this is the testimony: God has given us eternal life, and this life is in his Son. Whoever has the Son has life; whoever does not have the Son of God does not have life." I believe that in this context the word *eternal* refers to a true, full, real life as opposed to the facsimiles the world offers. As John writes in 5:20, "We know . . . that the Son of God has come and has given us understanding, so that we may know him who is true. And we are in him who is true by being in his Son Jesus Christ. He is the true God and eternal life." When Christ abides in us, and we abide in him, we enter into the very life of God; we enter into the communion of Father/Mother, Son, and Spirit; we enter into a life that is substantially more beautiful, joyful, peaceful. And we enter into life without end. Yes, we eventually die to this biological life we now reside in. Yet in relationship to the life of God, we never die.

Somehow, this eternal life begins even now. Jesus once made the astounding claim, "Very truly I tell you, whoever hears my word and believes him who sent me has eternal life and will not be judged but has crossed over [past tense!] from death to life. Very

6. Eugene Peterson, *The Message: The Bible in Contemporary Language*, Colorado Springs, CO: NavPress, 2004.

truly I tell you, a time is coming and has now come when the dead will hear the voice of the Son of God and those who hear will live" (John 5:24–25). The time has "now" come! The incarnation of Christ brought the eternal into time. T. S. Eliot wrote beautifully of this reality in the first of his *Four Quartets*, "Burnt Norton," calling the event of Christ's life "the still point of the turning world." Eliot continues:

> Neither from nor towards; at the still point, there the dance
>     is,
> But neither arrest nor movement. And do not call it fixity,
> Where past and future are gathered. Neither movement from
>     nor towards,
>   Neither ascent nor decline. Except for the point, the still
>     point,
> There would be no dance, and there is only the dance.[7]

I like that Eliot writes of "past" and "future" being "gathered," rather than destroyed or lost. A sense of time as a line doesn't cease to exist for those of us on this side of death. Rather, in Christ, that whole line gathers into our present experience.

God doesn't eliminate our understanding of time as linear, neither does God lift us up and out of this biological life and world. God enters into it in Jesus. John paints a graphic picture of this in 5:6: "This is the one who came by water and blood—Jesus Christ. He did not come by water only, but by water and blood." Water—Jesus' baptism. Blood—Jesus' crucifixion. These events anchor eternity in time. And within our lives, here and now, flash glimmers of this eternal life. Here, again, Eliot limns the mystery of this strange life, this time from the third of the "Four Quartets"—"The Dry Salvages":

>                                         To apprehend
>     The point of intersection of the timeless
>     With time, is an occupation for the saint—
>     No occupation either, but something given
>     And taken, in a lifetime's death in love,
>     Ardour, selflessness and self-surrender.

7. Eliot, *Collected Poems*, 177.

> For most of us, there is only the unattended
> Moment, the moment in and out of time,
> The distraction fit, lost in a shaft of sunlight,
> The wild thyme unseen, or the winter lightning
> Or the waterfall, or music heard so deeply
> That it is not heard at all, but you are the music
> While the music lasts. These are only hints and guesses,
> Hints followed by guesses; and the rest
> Is prayer, observance, discipline, thought and action.
> The hint half guessed, the gift half understood, is Incarna-
> tion.[8]

Though only half guessed, or half understood, this life incar-
nated in us has the power to transform everything for us, all that
we are and all that we do. John proclaims, "Everyone born of God
overcomes the world. This is the victory that has overcome the
world, even our faith" (5:4). The world is a place of death, hopeless-
ness, scarcity, meanness and violence whereas faith is filled with
life, hope, abundance, grace and peace. Every time we declare in
our hearts, "I believe in Jesus Christ, my Lord and Savior," we are
saying, "We can do better than this world offers."

In her empowering book *Receiving the Day*, Dorothy Bass
does much to help us live out this reality. In one passage, after re-
laying the story of how another author, Martin Marty, begins each
day by making the sign of the cross on his body, thereby reminding
him of his baptism, Bass writes:

> For all Christians, baptism embodies release from yester-
> day's sin and receipt of tomorrow's promise: going under
> the water the old self is buried in the death of Christ;
> rising from the water the self is new, joined to the resur-
> rected Christ . . . Freedom from bondage to the past and
> from fear for the future releases energies for bold and
> creative living, energies that might otherwise be directed
> to the destruction of self or others . . . Across the centu-
> ries, in countless languages and cultures, Christians have
> adopted shared patterns for speaking out loud the truth
> that this day is the day that God has made . . . a day in

8. Ibid, 198–199.

which we are invited to live in boldness and creativity . . .
Claiming the day as God's reminds us never to cede the
hours of our lives to the control of the powers of darkness and death.[9]

Bass reminds us that each day we have the opportunity to
rise to new life in Christ, freed from the grip of sin and its consequences, empowered to re-create our lives with God.

In a much older passage of writing Ezekiel shares with us an
even more vivid, and rightly well-known image of the source of
real life. As he looks out across a valley of dried bones, God prods
Ezekiel to prophesy to the bones that God will breathe life into
them. As Ezekiel follows God's leading, the bones begin to rattle
and join together. Ezekiel shares, "I looked, and tendons and flesh
appeared on them and skin covered them, but there was no breath
in them" (37:8). They looked alive, but it was merely a "clever fac-
simile," much like the facsimiles of life that our world presents to
us today. Then God prods Ezekiel to call in the "breath." Interestingly in both Hebrew and Greek, the words for "breath" and
"spirit" are the same! God's breath fills human bodies with true life.
Specifically, God prods Ezekiel to say, "Come from the four winds,
O breath, and breathe into these slain, that they may live" (37:9).
Again, Ezekiel shares, "So I prophesied as he commanded me, and
breath entered them; they came to life and stood up on their feet"
(37:10). God announces to Ezekiel that the bones are God's people
who have lost their way but that God has not given up on them.
Through Ezekiel, God promises to all the people, "I will put my
Spirit in you and you will live, and I will settle you in your own
land" (37:14). We believe, as followers of Christ, that God fulfilled
this promise through Jesus and the coming of the Holy Spirit.

In putting all these thoughts in writing, one of my wishes has
been that it might, at least in some small way, help even one person
see through the clever facsimiles of life and discover instead the
fullness of life in Christ. And so I close this chapter, and this book,
as seems appropriate, by adopting John's words as my own. As he
writes in 5:13, so too do I profess my hope, "I write these things

9. Bass, *Receiving the Day*, 20–21.

to you who believe in the name of the Son of God so that you may know that you have eternal life."

# Bibliography

Alford, Henry. "We Walk by Faith and Not by Sight." *The Presbyterian Hymnal: Hymns, Psalms, and Spiritual Songs*. Louisville, KY: Westminster/John Knox, 1990.

Augustine. *The Confessions: St. Augustine*. Translated by Maria Boulding. Preface by Patricia Hampl. Vintage Spiritual Classics. New York: Vintage, 1998.

Barclay, William. *The Letters of John and Jude*. Rev. ed. The Daily Bible Series. Philadelphia: Westminster, 1976. First published 1958 by Saint Andrew Press.

Bass, Dorothy C. *Receiving the Day: Christian Practices for Opening the Gift of Time*. San Francisco: Jossey-Bass, 2000.

Bellah, Robert N., et al. *Habits of the Heart: Individualism and Commitment in American Life*. Perennial Library. New York: Harper & Row, 1986.

Bernard of Clairvaux. *Talks on the Song of Songs*. Edited and modernized by Bernard Bangley. Brewster, MA: Paraclete, 2002.

Binns, Daniel. "Coffee Fanatic Admits Defeat After Failing to Visit Every Starbucks in the World." http://metro.co.uk/2014/05/19/coffee-fanatic-admits-defeat-after-failing-to-visit-every-starbucks-in-the-world-4733538/

Botton, Alain de. *The News: A User's Manual*. Vintage International Edition. New York: Random House, Vintage 2014.

Bragg, Rick. *All Over but the Shoutin*. New York: Vintage, 1997.

Brough, John, trans. *Poems from the Sanskrit*. New York: Penguin, 1968.

Buechner, Frederick. *Telling the Truth: The Gospel as Tragedy, Comedy, and Fairy Tale*. New York: Harper & Row, 1977.

Calvin, John. "Commentaries on the First Epistle of John." In *Commentaries on the Catholic Epistles*. Translated from the original Latin, and edited by John Owen. Vol. 22, *Calvin's Commentaries*. Grand Rapids, MI: Baker House, 1996. Originally printed for the Calvin Translation Society, Edinburgh.

Crabb, Larry. *Connecting: Healing for Ourselves and Our Relationships; A Radical New Vision*. Nashville, TN: W Group / Thomas Nelson, 1997

# Bibliography

Eliot, T. S. "Four Quartets." In *Collected Poems, 1909–1962*. New York: Harcourt Brace Javonovich, 1970.

Franklin, Benjamin. *The Autobiography of Benjamin Franklin*. Dover Thrift Editions. Mineola, NY: Dover, 1996.

Freudenrich, Craig, and William Harris. "How Light Works." http://science. howstuffworks.com/light.htm.

Gomes, Peter J. *Sermons: Biblical Wisdom for Daily Living*. New York: William Morrow, 1998.

Herbert, George. "Love (III)." In *George Herbert: The Country Parson, The Temple*. Edited, with an Introduction by John N. Wall, Jr. The Classics of Western Spirituality. New York: Paulist, 1981.

Ignatius. *The Spiritual Exercises of Saint Ignatius*. Translated and with commentary by Pierre Wolff. Ligouri, MO: Ligouri / Triumph, 1997.

Levertov, Denise. "St. Thomas Didymus." In *The Stream & the Sapphire: Selected Poems on Religious Themes*. New York: New Directions, 1997.

Medina, John. *The Outer Limits of Life*. Nashville, TN: Oliver–Nelson, 1991.

Palmer, Earl F. *1, 2, 3 John, Revelation*. Vol. 12, The Communicator's Commentary. Lloyd J. Ogilvie, general editor. Waco, TX: Word, 1982.

Reinhardt, Dave. "The Power and the Glory." http://transpositions.co.uk/the-power-and-the-glory.htm.

Rowling, J. K. *Harry Potter and the Sorcerer's Stone*. Illustrations by Mary Grandpré. New York: Scholastic, Arthur A. Levine, 1997.

Smith, D. Moody. *First, Second, and Third John*. Interpretation: A Bible Commentary for Teaching and Preaching. Louisville, KY: John Knox, 1991.

Steinbeck, John. *The Grapes of Wrath*. Chicago: J. G. Ferguson, 1939. Compass Books edition. New York: Viking, 1958.

Stodgill, Ron. "In the Line of Fire." *TIME*. August 24, 2002.

Stott, John. *The Letters of John*. Tyndale New Testament Commentaries 19. Reprint ed. Downers Grove, IL: IVP Academic, 2009.

Torrance, James B. *Worship, Community & the Triune God of Grace*. Downers Grove, IL: InterVarsity, 1996.

Turkle, Sherry. *Alone Together: Why We Expect More from Technology and Less from Each Other*. New York: Basic, 2011.